MONEY
TALES OF A WISE MAN

TOM GRANEAU

PUBLISH WRITERS
IMAGINING POSSIBILITIES

Disclaimer

⚜

This product is based mainly on imagination. While the book draws heavily from my professional experience, working with thousands of clients whose identities remain confidential, and my financial journey, which is also woven within this project, it is generally fiction. The names used are fictitious and are not intended to represent any specific individual beyond the characters in the story.

Dedication

If you're struggling with your finances, this book is dedicated to you. While you're not held blameless for your financial decisions or actions, realize that you, like most people, live in an economic system designed to keep you broke. You were born in it, trained by it, guided by it, and suffer the consequences of its ill intent. *Money Tales of a Wise Man* is written to inform you of our economic system, enlighten your path, and strengthen your resolve to become financially free, even with a small income.

Acknowledgment

I am deeply grateful to everyone who contributed to this project, from the editing, formatting, and printing—special thanks to those who provided guidance and emotional support.

Contents

❧

CHAPTER 1

❧

At the Bottom, Again

Pulling into the parking lot, John watched the early morning sun casting a golden hue over the sprawling complex - Superior Court of California. The courthouse, while large, had a modest and utilitarian feel, surrounded by a blend of palm trees and low-lying buildings typical of Southern California. With a heavy sigh, John glanced at the clock on the dashboard – nearly an hour before his scheduled session. Punctuality was something he valued deeply, and the thought of being late, especially for such a decisive event, always overwhelmed him with unease.

Exiting the car, John adjusted his tie nervously as his footsteps reverberated against the concrete while making his way toward the courthouse entrance. The memories of his previous bankruptcy lingered in the recesses of his mind, but he pushed them aside, focusing on the task at hand. He had to stay focused, but the burden of his financial troubles seemed to bear down on him with each step, and the anxiety of facing the trial gnawed at his insides.

As he entered the courtyard, he felt as if trepidation was injected directly into his heart, making his heart beat faster. The glass doors were locked, of course, and he felt like a lone warrior facing a slumbering monster.

1

John found a secluded spot near the entrance and leaned against the cool marble of the courthouse entrance. The courthouse had an unpretentious appearance, its beige and neutral tones blending with the surrounding environment, offering calmness despite the formality inside. His gaze drifted upwards, tracing the intricate patterns etched into the stone as a distraction from the impending proceedings. But despite his efforts to remain composed, his heart kept racing as if it was running for its life.

Soon, within minutes, two men arrived, and then two more and some more. John took a moment to survey the scene, observing the diverse array of faces – some resigned, others hopeful. Some shifted nervously on their feet, while others whispered anxiously to their trusted friends... or attorneys. The ones with their attorneys at their sides seemed to take solace in knowing they weren't alone in their hardships, while others, like John, had to face the daunting task alone as anxiety was evident on their faces. Alone or not, John was certain that they were united by the common dread of anxiety and uncertainty.

In an attempt to distract himself from his troubling thoughts, John looked at the gathering crowd around him and wondered what had brought them there. What were their stories? What had led them to that moment, standing in the courtyard of a courthouse? But the sight of them milling about only amplified his anxiety.

John's thoughts were soon interrupted by the sound of the clock hitting eight, signifying that the court would soon open and the hearing would commence. His heart skipped a beat as he realized the moment of truth had arrived. He took a deep breath, trying to steady his nerves as he prepared to face whatever lay beyond those imposing doors. With a hesitant step, he rejoined the throng of people making their way inside. A wave of panic swept over him as the echoes of footsteps and hushed conversations reverberated through the grand hallway, heightening his anticipation.

The heavy scent of piles of papers mixed with a subtle hint of anxiety lingered in the closed space. John looked around at people walking purposefully, with stacks of papers in hand and lines of worry etched on their faces, wondering if they were in a similar predicament.

Through the bustling, white corridors, he walked toward the courtroom assigned to them. It loomed before him like a daunting presence. His heart pounded as he stood outside, catching his breath as memories of past hardships resurfaced. A knot twisted in his stomach, tightening with each passing moment before he pushed open the doors.

John, along with a few others, walked into a sterile, modern space with clean lines and muted tones. The walls were paneled with light-colored wood, offset by sleek gray stone tiles that stretched behind the judge's bench. Two American flags stood proudly behind the bench. The atmosphere inside was solemn, the air heavy with the weight of impending judgment. They found seats, each silently preparing for what was to come.

As John looked around, he felt the room was well-lit, the fluorescent lights above casting a soft, clinical glow over them. The furniture was practical and functional—rows of dark chairs lined up neatly behind long wooden tables. The seating area, divided into sections, created an orderly sense of space. Two bailiffs stood watchfully at the front of the room, their eyes scanning the crowd, ready to provide directions or answer any questions. Their presence added to the sense of authority permeating the room, reminding everyone of the gravity of the proceedings.

After what felt like an eternity, the judge finally appeared, a figure of authority and wisdom clad in black robes. As he entered, a hush fell over the room, and everyone rose to their feet out of respect. Once the judge took his seat, they settled back down. A large seal on the wall behind the judge added a touch of solemnity to the space. John's eyes were fixed on the judge as he prepared to preside over the first case.

The tension in the room grew as the first case was called: "Ms. Julia Bakers. Come forward, please," the announcer's voice echoed through the hall.

John's heart rate quickened as he waited to see who was called. A woman, seemingly in her early 30s, rose from her seat and made her way to the front of the room.

The soft click of her stilettos against the carpeted floor echoed in the silence.

Reaching the podium with the microphone, she stood tall, her hands clasped in front of her, ready to face the questions or challenges the judge might present. There was a steely determination in her gaze. Beside her stood a man in a full suit, presumably her lawyer.

The judge peered down from the bench, his gaze shrewd yet impartial. "Ms. Bakers," he began, his voice commanding attention, "please state your name and the nature of your petition."

Julia cleared her throat. Her voice was steady as she responded, "My name is Julia Bakers, Your Honor, and I am petitioning for Chapter 7 bankruptcy."

John watched with bated breath as the proceedings unfolded, his nerves raw and frayed.

The judge nodded. "And what led you to file for bankruptcy, Ms. Bakers?"

Julia met his gaze without flinching. "I incurred significant medical expenses due to an unforeseen illness, Your Honor, which left me unable to work for an extended period."

The judge listened attentively, his brow furrowing slightly. "I see. And have you made any efforts to repay your debts?"

"Yes, Your Honor," Julia replied. "I have explored various options for debt repayment, but unfortunately, my circumstances have made it impossible to meet my financial obligations."

The judge deliberated briefly before making his decision. "Based on the evidence presented, I rule in favor of Ms. Bakers. You are hereby relieved of your financial obligations."

As Julia turned to leave, her eyes sparkled with gratitude and relief, knowing she was finally free from her debts. John felt a sense of admiration as she exited the courtroom. Despite the daunting nature of the proceedings, she had faced the judge with poise and dignity. With renewed determination, John braced himself for his own turn, ready to confront the challenge ahead.

As the cases progressed, time inched forward, and the moment John had been dreading finally arrived. His case number was called: "Mr. John Aaden, come forward, please." The announcement broke through the silence of the courtroom like a thunderclap. With a deep breath, he rose from his seat, his legs unsteady beneath him.

Walking toward the front of the room, each step felt heavier than the last, as though he were carrying the weight of the world on his shoulders. The eyes of everyone in the room seemed to bore into him, their silent scrutiny adding to the pressure of the moment.

Reaching the stand, John felt his palms grow sweaty as he gripped the edges tightly. The microphone loomed before him, a stark reminder of the gravity of the situation. He took a moment to gather his thoughts, steeling himself for the questions and judgments to come.

"Please state your name and the nature of your petition," the judge's voice boomed through the courtroom.

"I am John Aaden, Your Honor, and I am petitioning for... Chapter 7 bankruptcy," he replied, his voice steady despite the knot of apprehension tightening in his stomach.

"Mr. Aaden," the judge began, his tone authoritative, "I have reviewed your case, and I noticed you had a prior bankruptcy discharge about twelve years ago. The circumstances of this case are very similar to the previous one. Is that correct?"

John's heart sank as the judge mentioned his prior bankruptcy. A wave of anxiety crashed over him, pulling him back into a painful past he had hoped to leave behind. He had prayed his past financial hardships would remain hidden, but now the thought of exposing this vulnerability filled him with embarrassment.

"Yes, Your Honor," John replied hesitantly, his voice tinged with resignation and regret. He had hoped for a different outcome, but now it seemed his past choices were coming back to haunt him.

As the judge read through his financial history, uncertainty flooded John's mind. He couldn't help but wonder how the knowledge of his prior bankruptcy would influence the current case. Would it be seen as a pattern of financial irresponsibility? Doubt swirled within him, leaving him feeling helpless in the face of impending judgment.

He had hoped to leave this chapter of his life behind, but finding himself back in bankruptcy court only twelve years after his previous discharge left John questioning his decisions and feeling trapped in an unbreakable cycle of financial turmoil. Shame and disappointment gnawed at him, threatening to consume him.

When John began to speak, his voice wavered slightly, betraying his nerves. But with each word, he felt a growing sense of determination to speak his truth and defend his case: "I understand, Your Honor, but I assure you, the circumstances surrounding my current financial situation are entirely different from those of my previous bankruptcy. Since then, I have diligently worked to rebuild my financial stability, but unforeseen challenges have once again led me to seek the protection of the court."

The judge listened intently as John laid out his arguments, his expression unreadable. His piercing gaze scrutinized John, searching for any signs of deception or evasion.

"What steps have you taken to address your financial difficulties this time, Mr. Aaden?" the judge inquired, his voice measured yet probing.

"I have sought financial counseling and explored all available options for debt repayment," John replied earnestly. "I have also made concerted efforts to increase my income and reduce unnecessary expenses, but despite my best efforts, the burden of debt has become overwhelming."

John answered the judge's questions honestly and thoroughly, hoping his words would sway the decision in his favor. But as the proceedings drew to a close, uncertainty hung in the air. All John could do was wait, his heart pounding as he braced himself for whatever future lay ahead. Standing in the courtroom, John was a picture of depression and disappointment. His eyes reflected his wish to be anywhere but there, far from the harsh reality of his financial problems. Although he held himself together emotionally, his inner chaos was evident in the way he clutched his hands tightly, his knuckles white.

Memories of his first bankruptcy resurfaced, reopening old wounds. San Diego, California. That was where it all unraveled before, where his life had been upended by unfortunate events. Losing his job had been the catalyst, setting off a chain reaction of financial turmoil. His steady income faltered, leading to the gut-wrenching ordeal of losing his home to foreclosure.

Credit card debt had become a constant companion, a source of unrelenting stress. The relentless phone calls and letters from creditors had haunted him, a persistent reminder of his financial shortcomings. Now, standing in the courtroom once again, John faced bankruptcy for the second time.

The dull atmosphere around him reflected the gravity of the situation. The air was stale and heavy with anxiety and uncertainty. Lawyers and the judge shuffled about, detached from his problem, magnifying his loneliness. John was painfully aware that he was responsible for everything that had happened.

He couldn't help but wonder if this cycle would repeat a third time. The fear of another downfall gnawed at his spirit, leaving him uncertain about his ability to overcome the challenges ahead.

Taking a deep breath, John tried to steady his nerves. Regardless of the judge's verdict, the path forward might be lined with obstacles, but he refused to succumb entirely to despair. Gathering the fragments of hope that remained, he knew his fight for financial redemption was far from over.

Nevertheless, the weight of the reality remained: roughly twelve years since his last encounter with bankruptcy, and now, at forty-nine years old, life had led him back to the same place he had been a decade ago. The emotional toll of facing financial ruin for the second time was immense, leaving him feeling defeated and helpless.

After what felt like an eternity of tense anticipation, the judge cleared his throat, breaking through the heavy silence that engulfed the room and capturing my attention. John felt a surge of nervous energy coursing through him as he awaited the verdict that would shape his future.

With a measured tone, the judge began delivering the news, "After careful consideration and review of the case, I have decided to discharge Mr. John Aden's case of bankruptcy, based on..."

But John barely heard the rest of the judge's words. His heart pounded in his chest, drowning out everything else as a rush of adrenaline flooded his veins. Discharged. The word echoed in his mind like a mantra, disbelief washing over him in waves. Relief gushed in him like a stream of fresh water, leaving him feeling light-headed and dizzy with gratitude. It was as if a weight had been lifted from his shoulders, freeing him from the suffocating grip of financial uncertainty.

As the judge went on to explain the conditions of the discharge, John listened intently, his mind racing with the possibilities that lay ahead. The knowledge that creditors could no longer pursue him for discharged debts filled him with liberation he hadn't felt in years.

After ensuring that he understood the discharge conditions and had no further questions, the judge made a ruling for the case to be discharged and closed. With a heartfelt thank you to the judge, John felt a renewed sense of hope and optimism for the future.

Walking out of the courtroom, a weightless feeling settled over him, accompanied by a profound sense of gratitude. The sun seemed to shine a little brighter; the air felt a little sweeter as John stepped out into the world, ready to embark on a new chapter of his life.

John was finally free from the shackles of debt once more, and now he hoped not to succumb to the same fate again.

CHAPTER 2

❧

Where is the Gold?

Nineteen-year-old John, with dreams as vast as the Caribbean Sea, stood on the sidewalk of Kingston, Jamaica. Wearing his headphones, his eyes closed as he surrendered to the rhythmic beats of "Only in America" by Jay and the Americans. The music enveloped him like a comforting embrace, transporting him to a place of boundless possibilities.

John's head swayed to the beat as he sang along to the lyrics, "Only in America/ Can a guy from anywhere/ Go to sleep a pauper and wake up a millionaire/ Only in America/ Can a kid without a cent/ Get a break and maybe grow up to be President/ Only in America/ Land of opportunity, yeah/ Would a classy girl like you fall for a poor boy like me...."

With each word he sang, he envisioned himself standing tall amidst the towering skyscrapers of America's cities and his name emblazoned on the walls of fame for all to see. The song had become his anthem to live by; to him, America was a treasure chest of wealth and prosperity. In his mind's eye, he saw streets paved with gold, gleaming under the radiant sun, pulling him to chase his dreams and carve out his path to success.

Lost in his reverie, John felt exhilaration course through him, fueling his motivation to turn his fantasies into reality. For in that moment, amidst the pulsating rhythm of the music, he believed with certainty that America held the key to unlocking a future beyond his wildest dreams. That evening, as he met his friends in The Deck, John's voice rang out excitedly, "You know, guys, my brother, Nathan, in America, he's sending back money every month to our family. He and his family are living like kings over there! I can't wait to go and see it for myself."

His friends leaned in closer as their interest was piqued by John's tales. "Wow, John, that's incredible!" exclaimed Tony, his eyes widening in awe. "You know my aunt in New York? She's got this big house with a swimming pool and everything. They're living the high life over there!"

Nods of agreement rippled through the group as they exchanged eager glances, each one eager to share their tales of relatives living lavishly in America. "Yeah, man, America is where it's at," chimed in Stacy, "My cousin in Los Angeles has got this fancy car collection and a mansion overlooking the ocean. It's like something out of a movie!"

Laughter erupted among the friends as they indulged in fantasies of luxurious lifestyles and opulent surroundings. Marcus exclaimed, "My uncle lives in Miami, and he has a yacht that's bigger than some hotels here. They're practically living on a permanent vacation! Imagine that, eh? We can be rolling in riches, too!"

The belief that America held the key to unlocking their dreams beat in their hearts. "One day, we'll make it there, just like our relatives," declared Ricardo, "And when we do, we'll show them what we're made of."

After months of toiling day and night, John's determination finally bore fruit. Each dawn saw him rise with the sun, ready to embark on another day of hard work. From delivering newspapers in the early hours to taking on extra shifts at the local market, John spared no effort in his quest to save enough money to leave for America. His parents also supported him, contributing what they could to help him achieve his dream. They harbored dreams and aspirations of their own, envisioning a future where their son's success would bring prosperity and fortune to their family.

As the days melted into weeks and the weeks morphed into months, John was caught in preparation to travel to America. His days were filled with determination as he worked tirelessly, saving every penny he could muster. Each dollar added to his growing stash felt like a small step toward his dreams.

Finally, the long-awaited news arrived. Nathan, his older brother residing in El Cajon, had come through with a plan to pave the way for John's enrollment in a private high school associated with his local church. The prospect of embarking on this new chapter of his life filled John with uncontainable joy and excitement.

With Nathan's guidance and support, John swiftly took the necessary steps to secure his place at the high school his brother had chosen. Applications were filled out, and the daunting paperwork for the student visa was carefully completed. Each task completed brought him one step closer to his ultimate goal of leaving behind the broken, patchy streets of Kingston for the promise of a brighter future in America.

As he waited for the approval of his visa, John's anticipation bubbled over. His mind raced with visions of the opportunities that awaited him in his new home. He imagined the sprawling campus of the high school, with its ivy-covered buildings and bustling student life - a far cry from the streets of Kingston that had been his reality for so long.

When the day arrived, he stood at the airport gate with excitement and nervousness coursing through his veins. Boarding the plane bound for San Diego, California, in the US, John's heart raced. As he settled into his seat, he marveled at the magnitude of the moment. The hum of the engines, the scent of recycled air, and the gentle vibration of the aircraft all made him look forward to the 'roads paved with gold.'

Looking out the window, John watched as the familiar sights of Kingston faded into the distance, replaced by the vast expanse of the sky. With each passing mile, he felt liberation fill him, knowing that he was finally on his way to the land of opportunity – America.

As the airplane touched down at San Diego International Airport, formerly known as Lindbergh Field, John's heart pounded with excitement. He stepped out of the airport, and the warm California breeze welcomed him, along with his brother, Nathan, whose face lit up as soon as he saw John.

"John! You've grown so much!" Nathan exclaimed, pulling his brother into a warm embrace.

John's heart swelled with joy as he embraced his brother, feeling a rush of gratitude for Nathan's presence. "I've missed you, Nathan," he admitted as his voice choked with emotion.

"I've missed you too, little brother," he replied with a weary smile tugging at the corners of his lips.

As they made their way to the parking lot, Nathan hoisted John's suitcase effortlessly, but John couldn't help but notice the tired lines etched on his brother's face, who was just in his 40s.

"Are you okay, Nathan?" John asked, concern lacing his words. "You look tired."

Nathan chuckled wearily, "Just the usual grind, John. Don't worry about me; I'll be fine."

John's excitement for being in San Diego overshadowed any concern he might have had for his brother's tiredness, prompting him to let the matter go and immerse himself fully in the experience of being in the vibrant city by the sea.

As they approached the parking lot, John's eyes scanned the rows of cars, expecting to see something luxurious. However, as Nathan pressed the button on his key, a car's lights blinked. John's gaze fell upon the battered sedan, its paint peeling and headlights dim. Disappointment struck John as he realized the reality of their situation.

"Is this... our ride?" John asked, trying to mask his disappointment.

Nathan nodded sheepishly, "Yeah, she's not much to look at, but she gets us where we need to go."

Nathan laid John's suitcase into the trunk before sliding into the driving seat. The engine coughed and sputtered to life as Nathan turned the key. Despite John's initial excitement about starting a new life in America, he couldn't shake off the sinking feeling in his chest as he slid into the passenger seat.

"Welcome to the States, John!" Nathan's grin was infectious, but John felt a pang of sadness for his brother. As they merged onto the freeway, John glanced out the window, taking in the sights of the unfamiliar city. Towering skyscrapers punctuated the skyline; their glass facades glinted in the sunlight. As they drove through downtown San Diego, John marveled at the bustling streets stretching out before them. While lush green parks dotted the cityscape here and there, nestled amidst the towering buildings, they offered pockets of nature's serenity amidst the urban hustle and bustle.

Traversing the streets of San Diego before getting home, John marveled at the diversity of the city. Throngs of people rushed along the sidewalks, and their faces were a mosaic of different ethnicities and backgrounds. But as they reached El Cajon, John's thoughts turned inward, his gaze lingering on the familiar sights that seemed to resemble those of his hometown in Kingston, Jamaica. As they reached El Cajon, John's initial excitement waned, and a sense of familiarity filled him. The scenes unfolding before him bore a striking resemblance to those of his hometown in Kingston, Jamaica. The streets, narrower and the buildings smaller, felt all too familiar. Even though there were supermarkets, the local farmers had set up small sheds here and there to sell their produce.

"Maybe there are some roads here that are paved with gold among those big buildings," he mused to himself optimistically.

Nathan stopped his car in front of what John hoped would be a luxury neighborhood. However, as he stood in front of the old, rusty door of an apartment building, his hopes began to fade again. Pushing open the creaking door, John was greeted by the sight of peeling paint and cracked walls. The carpeted floors looked faded, the furniture worn, and the air heavy with the smell of dampness. John's heart sank. This was not the lavish mansion he had imagined. Instead, it was a cramped space filled with used furniture and worn belongings.

He was immediately greeted by Nathan's wife, Lola, who wore a weary smile despite evidence of fatigue on her face. She cradled a fussy baby in her arms, gently rocking him back and forth in a futile attempt to soothe his cries. Meanwhile, their eldest child, a seven-year-old boy, Jason, played with old, used toys strewn across the worn-out carpet in the living room.

"Hey there, John. Welcome," Lola greeted him.

"Hi, Lola," John replied, "Need any help with him?" He gestured toward the baby.

Lola shook her head, but her eyes reflected gratitude, "Thanks, John, but I've got it. Nathan's just putting away your things. Make yourself comfortable."

As Nathan returned from placing John's belongings in a room for him to stay, he scooped up the crying baby. His movements were instinctively gentle as he murmured soothing words in his ear. "There, there, little man. Daddy's got you," Nathan cooed. Slowly but surely, the infant's sobs subsided, replaced by soft whimpers as he snuggled in his father's arms.

Meanwhile, Lola disappeared into the kitchen, likely preparing a meal for the family amidst the chaos of their cramped apartment. John watched the tender exchange between father and son, a pang of guilt tugging at his heart as he took in the tired faces of his brother and sister-in-law. John couldn't shake the feeling of disillusionment. The couch in the living room sagged a little, the curtains showed signs of wear, and some kitchen tiles were chipped and stained. The view was far from the luxurious accommodations he had envisioned.

"I know it's not what you imagined," Nathan began, sensing John's thoughts. "But this is all we can afford right now. You can share Jason's room... I have already set up a separate bed—it's only a two-room apartment, and rent is quite expensive." Conversation flowed awkwardly as Nathan went on to explain their struggles with debts and financial hardships. "It's tough out here, John. We're just trying to make ends meet," he admitted with a weary sigh.

Sitting on the worn-out couch, John couldn't help but feel a pang of disappointment at the reality of their situation. The lines on Nathan's face were the evidence of countless hours spent working day and night to make ends meet. Dark circles shadowed his eyes, betraying the exhaustion that burdened him heavily. His shoulders slumped with weariness, and his movements were slow and labored. Despite his best efforts to hide it, the strain of their difficult circumstances was evident in his weary sigh and faltering step.

"Why do you send money back to Jamaica if you're struggling here?" John asked.

Nathan let out a tired sigh, and his shoulders sagged. "A few American dollars go a long way when converted to Jamaican dollars," he explained. "It might not seem like much here, but back home, it means a lot to our family. It's enough to make them happy for a while." He paused, a weary expression crossing his face. "But here, everything is so expensive," Nathan continued, "I have to sacrifice a lot of my own needs just to get by. It's like being stuck in a rat hole, fighting for that one chickpea."

John nodded in understanding, though disappointment still lingered in his heart. He knew his brother was doing his best in a difficult situation. With a heavy sigh, he resolved to keep his feelings to himself, not wanting to burden Nathan any further. After all, they were family, and they would find a way to support each other through thick and thin. After spending some time with his brother, John excused himself and made his way to the bathroom. Sitting on the old, cheap toilet seat, he couldn't shake the feeling of disappointment and disillusionment. The America he had dreamed of seemed a world away from the reality he now faced.

John quickly gathered himself together and put on a brave smile as he returned to the living room and settled onto the couch. Lola, his sister-in-law, bustled around, setting a simple meal for four at the weathered dining table. Nathan asked him to join them. As they ate, John couldn't shake off the sinking feeling in his stomach. The meal was no better than what they had in Jamaica, and the taste of disappointment lingered on his tongue.

After dinner, John excused himself for some fresh air, stepping out onto the balcony. Across the way, he observed their neighbors going about their evening routines - a woman hanging clothes, her weary expression mirroring Lola's exhaustion.

Longing for a sense of escape, John decided to go out for a walk. He walked a few blocks in El Cajon. His every step was a desperate attempt to make sense of his new reality. As he passed by shops and stalls, he noticed people pulling out their credit cards to pay. He did not have one, so he only watched from the sidelines. With disappointment and heaviness in his heart, he went back to his brother's apartment.

The following weekend, Nathan drove John through an affluent neighborhood, eager to show him where the rich people lived. "Check out this area, man. It's where dreams come true," Nathan remarked. This is what people did occasionally, calling this activity 'Dream building' to set their expectations higher than what they currently have.

John and Nathan cruised through the picturesque streets of Fletcher Hills El Cajon, marveling at the lush greenery and well-maintained homes that lined their path. John observed in silence as they drove through the neighborhood.

"Man, I always forget how beautiful this neighborhood is. It's like a little slice of paradise tucked away in San Diego," Nathan mused, breaking the silence.

John only nodded in agreement as his eyes scanned the scenery with admiration. The sun dipped low in the sky, casting a glow over the rolling hills and lush greenery that stretched as far as the eye could see.

As they rounded a bend, Nathan pointed excitedly toward a group of hikers making their way along a trail that wound through the hills, "Check it out, John! Look at all those people out enjoying the trails."

John nodded, his gaze following the path of the hikers as they disappeared into the tree line. He could feel the yearning for such simple joys in his brother's tone. They continued, passing by charming homes nestled among the trees, each one adding to the neighborhood's unique character. Luxurious cars were neatly parked in front of these homes; they were a stark contrast to the dilapidated sedan that Nathan drove. From quaint cottages with colorful gardens blooming in the front yard to sleek modern designs, the architecture reflected the diverse community that called Fletcher Hills home. As they passed by, John's gaze lingered on the extravagant displays of wealth, filling him with a bitter sense of resentment. "This is what you should have, bro," John muttered, almost to himself, unaware of the storm of emotions brewing within him.

As they approached a bustling shopping district, John glanced at the clock on the dashboard. "Looks like we'll have to come back another time to explore all the shops and restaurants. Traffic's starting to pick up," Nathan smiled as they navigated through the congestion, knowing that the slight inconvenience was a small price to pay for the privilege of living in such a remarkable neighborhood.

Upon arriving back at Nathan's tiny apartment, John felt the defeat settle upon him. The harsh reality of their situation burdened his mind - the disparity between the haves and the have-nots looming large in his thoughts.

Sitting down for dinner with his brother's family, John remained silent as disappointment overwhelmed his stream of thought. Later, as he lay on the creaking bed, Jason was already fast asleep on his own bed nearby. John's thoughts drifted to the divide between the privileged and the struggling. "What separates them from us?" he pondered silently.

In the quiet darkness of the room, this thought gnawed at him, "What made some people live in mansions while others barely scraped by?" It was a question that John knew he wouldn't find an easy answer to, but one that he couldn't shake off.

Perplexed and disheartened, John found himself again questioning his once-idyllic vision of America. "Where's the gold? Where's the wealth?" he asked himself.

There was only silence that lingered in response.

Sitting up, John rubbed his temples as he tried to make sense of it all. "This life isn't much better than where I came from," he muttered to himself as disappointment crept in. He had believed America to be a land of endless opportunity and wealth, but now he realized that it wasn't quite what he had imagined.

With a heart now brimming with sorrow, John knew that he needed to make changes in his own life. Inspired by the wealthy individuals he had encountered in Jamaica, on television, and here in San Diego, he harbored dreams of achieving similar success. But he also recognized that he needed education to turn those dreams into reality.

"I need to educate myself," John resolved as despair turned into determination, flashing in his eyes, "I want to be wealthy, like those people I've seen. I need to take steps to improve my life." With his decision firm in his mind, John embarked on a new journey. Despite not having a high school diploma, he was determined to earn his GED, knowing it was the first step toward a brighter future. As John walked the streets of America, he found comfort in the abundance of choices and opportunities that surrounded him – from the variety of supermarkets to the endless options for food, fun, and leisure. But he knew that in America, money played a big part in accessing those opportunities. Without it, life could be tough. He saw how money could open doors and provide a better life.

Every day, John took small but meaningful steps toward his goals. He poured over textbooks and study guides to study hard for his GED while attending high school, driven by the hope of achieving the wealth and success he dreamed of.

Two years later, John finally held his GED certificate in his hands - a tangible symbol of his hard work and determination, and discontinued the high school. The sense of accomplishment that rushed over him was apparent as he realized he was one step closer to achieving his goals.

But John's journey didn't end there. Shortly after receiving his GED, he found himself falling in love with Chandice, a kindred spirit from the Caribbean who shared his dreams of a better life. Their love blossomed quickly, and before long, they were planning a future together.

They moved into a modest one-bedroom apartment. It was small and humble, but to John, it was temporary. His dreams were bigger than that. One year later, their world was transformed once again with the arrival of their baby daughter, Grace. She was a tiny bundle of joy; her laughter filled his heart with warmth and light. As John cradled his newborn daughter, Grace, in his arms, he felt an overwhelming sense of responsibility fill him. Here, in the cozy confines of their one-bedroom apartment, surrounded by the ones he loved most, he made a silent vow to provide her with a life very different from his own.

As he gazed down at her tiny, sleeping form, John's mind swirled with dreams of a bright and prosperous future. He imagined Grace growing up in a world filled with opportunity and abundance, where her every need and desire would be met without hesitation. He pictured her in a lavish room adorned with plush furnishings and delicate decorations, a space fit for a princess. Her laughter would echo through the halls.

But it wasn't just material possessions that John dreamed of providing for Grace. He longed to offer her a life rich in experiences and opportunities where she could pursue her passions and fulfill her dreams without restraint. Whether it was traveling the world, pursuing higher education, or chasing her wildest ambitions, John vowed to support her every step of the way.

As for transportation, John imagined Grace cruising down the streets in her very own luxurious car, the wind in her hair and a smile on her face. It would be a symbol of her independence and success. As he looked at Chandice cradling little Grace, John felt a renewed sense of purpose and determination coursing through his veins. With his wife by his side, he knew that anything was possible.

CHAPTER 3

❦

A Call for Service

John, now 24 years old, stood in the queue of RSS El Cajon as the rays of the afternoon sun gleamed at the concrete courtyard. The banners, with depictions of heroic Marines in action, flapped gently in the breeze. The place looked alive with the hum of conversations as recruits exchanged nervous jokes and words of encouragement. Soldiers in crisp uniforms stood sentry as if their presence was a reminder of the path that lay ahead for those who dared to tread it.

Taking a deep breath, John approached the reception desk and handed over his documents. His GED certificate, earned through nights of study and perseverance, felt like a ticket to a brighter future.

The recruiter, a stern-faced man, reviewed John's papers with a nod of approval. His clean criminal record was a relief. With a curt motion, the recruiter handed him a form to fill out, and John set to work. His hand was steady despite the fluttering in his stomach.

As he finished filling out the form, the recruiter informed him of the date and location for the ASVAB and his MEPS medical exam test. John nodded. He knew this was just the first step on the new path ahead, but he was ready to prove himself. Soon, the day of the test arrived, and John had poured over his study materials with a fervor born of desperation. He knew that this test would decide his future, and failure was not an option. After attempting the CAT-ASVAB, John proceeded through a series of rigorous assessments to ensure he met the physical requirements of military service. First, he underwent height and weight measurements, standing tall as the tape measure snaked around him, ensuring he met the strict standards set by the military.

Next came the hearing and vision examinations, where John sat in a dim room, headphones clamped over his ears as he strained to hear the faintest of tones. The optometrist scrutinized his eyes, testing his vision to the letter, ensuring he possessed the keen eyesight necessary for the trials ahead.

Urine and blood tests followed. John, providing samples with solemnity, knew that these tests would not reveal any underlying health issues that could affect his ability to serve. The drug and alcohol tests were a formality, but John submitted to them willingly, understanding the importance of maintaining a clean and sober lifestyle in the military.

With each test completed, John felt the expectation upon him, knowing that he needed to prove himself not just mentally but physically fit for duty. Muscle group and joint maneuvers came next. John stripped down to his underwear and underwent a series of simple flexibility and balance tests. He moved with precision and grace, and his body responded to the commands with ease. Following that, a complete physical examination and interview awaited him. The medical officer probed and prodded, asking questions about his medical history and any past injuries. John answered honestly, and his resolve shone through as he recounted his journey to this point. As he emerged from the final examination room, John felt pride. He had passed every test thrown his way, proving himself not just mentally sharp but physically capable of meeting the demands of military service.

After a few days, the letter arrived in the mail, and he breathed a sigh of relief when he saw his score: 72, above the average. It was more than perfect to move forward. The location for his boot camp was also mentioned: San Diego, Marine Corps Recruit Depot. A flow of excitement coursed through him as he realized that he was one step closer to his dream of service. Finally, he had a purpose and the opportunity to earn the coveted title that all those uniformed Americans possessed. With his head held high and his gaze fixed firmly on the future, John knew that his journey was just beginning. He was filled with hope, determination, and a steadfast belief that he would indeed find his American gold in the Marine Corps.

Just as John prepared to leave for his recruit training, he was blessed with his second child – a son. With Chandice, he decided to call him Damien. He longed to spend precious moments with his growing family, but the looming prospect of recruit training demanded his undivided attention.

Now, he stood at the gates of the Marine Corps Recruit Depot San Diego, observing as the sun beat down on the sprawling compound. As he approached the entrance, the sight of the iconic eagle, globe, and anchor insignia emblazoned on the gate filled him with pride and purpose. He stepped inside, and the thick air, with the sound of marching boots and the distinct scent of discipline and determination, gave him goosebumps. He watched the rows of uniformed Marines move with precision.

As he stepped onto the yellow footprints, he felt the significance of the moment. It was a moment of transition - his official entry into the world of the United States Marine Corps. The yellow footprints, worn smooth by the countless recruits who had stood upon them before him, served as a solemn reminder of the legacy he was now a part of.

John's journey from the initial letter to the moment he stood on the yellow footprints took about five months. The transformation from Poolee to Recruit was symbolic for him as it was a shedding of one identity in favor of another. Some might see it as a demotion, a stripping away of individuality until only the essence of a Marine remained. But to John, it was a badge of honor in return for his commitment to something greater than himself.

With only a week before training commenced, John cherished every fleeting second with Chandice, Grace, and his newborn Damien. His heart swelled with pride at the thought of providing for his loved ones, but the separation was inevitable. As he bid farewell to his family and stepped onto the hallowed grounds of this recruit training center, John steeled himself for the rigorous journey ahead. The thirteen-week process loomed large, during which the recruit became cut off from the civilian world and had to adapt to a Marine Corps lifestyle. This is what happened to John. Amidst the extensive expanse of the Marine Corps training grounds, the days blurred together in a blur of sweat, fatigue, and determination. From the early morning reveille to the lights-out call at night, every moment was filled with challenges designed to push John and his fellow recruits to their limits and beyond. They underwent rigorous instruction covering a wide array of subjects such as weapons proficiency, the Marine Corps Martial Arts Program, personal hygiene, close order drill, and Marine Corps history. The emphasis was on physical fitness, with recruits required to meet a minimum standard through the Physical Fitness Test to graduate.

While the physical demands were taxing, the mental fortitude aspect proved most challenging for John. However, he recognized its transformative power, not just in becoming a better person overall but also in becoming the Marine he aspired to be. Following instructions was crucial, as deviating could result in being singled out for criticism, as John observed within his platoon.

Physically, John had to adapt to running several miles without dropping out of formation, a feat he had never attempted before boot camp. Initially, he assumed the gradual approach to running distances was manageable, only to realize that consistent 5 to 7-mile runs were the norm. Witnessing the consequences for those who couldn't keep up and received the blanket party motivated him to push beyond his limits, highlighting the importance of mental resilience. He adhered to the demanding exercise regimen, striving to meet expectations, whether it was completing 80 to 100 sit-ups, 20 pull-ups, or enduring prolonged push-up sessions, reinforcing the significance of discipline and mental attitude in achieving success in such demanding circumstances.

Between classes, John also had to meet minimum combat-oriented swimming qualifications while wearing gear, qualify in rifle marksmanship with the M16A4 service rifle, and prepare to complete a grueling 54-hour simulated combat exercise known as 'The Crucible.'

One of the toughest weeks for John was 'The March.' It involved carrying all his gear, a 70-pound pack, canteens full of water that he couldn't drink until instructed, and his M-16, all while enduring what's called a forced march. Split into two files along a dirt road, they marched up and down hills between field classes. Despite the physical strain, these sessions offered thrilling experiences like learning camouflage techniques, grenade handling, hand-to-hand combat, and low crawling under barbed wire amidst live fire.

Sleeping under the stars in his sleeping bag during the week-long adventure was refreshing, but the schedule compression due to Christmas made it more challenging. With four days' worth of tasks crammed into Monday through Wednesday, the forced march became even more grueling. The formation stretched out over a mile, and recruits had to maintain proximity. When the command came to 'Reach up and grab a hold,' John and his fellow recruits responded in unison, 'Aye, Aye, Sir,' making for a chaotic scene with everyone trying to maintain the required distance. Then, there came the infamous gas chamber. Recruits were first taught how to use their gas masks, then subjected to exercises to induce heavy breathing. One by one, they were made to remove their masks, open their eyes, and recite general orders before being exposed to gas. Afterward, they had to clear their masks and endure the discomfort as some recruits struggled with the effects of the gas, choking and gagging.

After leaving the depot, John went on the field training at Edson Range aboard Marine Corps Base Camp Pendleton. The experience was immersive, as he honed his skills on the rifle range, engaged in field exercises, and faced the ultimate test in the Crucible.

The grueling 54-hour culmination exercise pushed John to his limits both physically and mentally. Enduring fatigue, hunger, and relentless challenges, he drew upon his training and determination to persevere, emerging stronger and more resilient than before.

Returning to MCRD San Diego for Marine Week and graduation, John felt a surge of pride and emotion. Amidst the sea of people, he spotted his wife Chandice and their daughter Grace, whose presence filled him with joy and gratitude. Seeing his son, now 13 months old, he marveled at how much he had grown during his time away, realizing the sacrifices both he and his family had made for him to become a Marine. As he stood tall on the parade ground, surrounded by his loved ones and fellow Marines, John felt a sense of accomplishment. With the support of his family and the bonds forged with his brothers and sisters in arms, he knew he was ready to embrace the challenges and responsibilities of serving as a United States Marine.

John quickly began as a Private (E-1), earning a basic Marine active-duty salary of $20,792 per year. Graduating from basic training marked the beginning of his service but also the start of his financial struggles. With a young family to support, John found it challenging to make ends meet on his entry-level pay.

However, driven by ambition and determination, John diligently worked toward advancement. After six months of dedicated service, he earned a promotion to

Private First Class (E-2), boosting his annual income to $23,310. This increase provided some relief, but finances remained tight as he balanced his responsibilities as a Marine with the expenses of his daughter, now in a private school.

Undeterred, John continued to excel in his duties, demonstrating leadership and commitment. His hard work paid off when, after nine months of service, he achieved the rank of Lance Corporal (E-3). This promotion came with a higher salary range of $24,512.40 to $27,633.60 per year, offering John a more stable financial footing.

Despite his growing income, John still faced financial challenges. The modest increase in income wasn't enough to offset the rising costs of maintaining a household and supporting his growing family. One evening, as John sat at the kitchen table with his wife Chandice, surrounded by bills and financial statements, he couldn't help but express his frustration. "I just don't understand it, Chandice," he sighed, running a hand through his hair, "I'm working hard, climbing the ranks, but it feels like we're barely staying afloat."

Chandice reached across the table, gently squeezing his hand. "I know, John. We're doing our best," she replied, "But with the mortgage, the kids' expenses, and everything else, it's tough."

John nodded as his brow furrowed in deep thought. "Yeah, and then there's the credit card debt," he admitted reluctantly. "I never imagined it would be this difficult, especially with all the sacrifices I've made."

Their conversation was interrupted by the sound of their daughter Grace's laughter echoing from the living room. John glanced in that direction as a soft smile tugged at the corners of his lips. "I just want to give them the best life possible," he murmured. Chandice reached for his hand again, offering a reassuring squeeze. "And you will, John. We'll get through this together," she said reassuringly.

Despite the financial struggles, John's commitment to his military duties never wavered. He continued to excel in his role, driven by a sense of duty to his country and a desire to provide for his family. Yet, as he marched forward in his career, the question loitered in the back of his mind: Where was the promised land of opportunity, the American gold, the American dream that seemed just out of reach despite his relentless efforts?

CHAPTER 4

⸎

A New Reality

After dedicating eight years to military service, John found himself at a crossroads. Despite his commitment, financial stability remained a far-fetched dream. Each year of service seemed to offer diminishing returns. Frustrated and yearning for a better future, John made the difficult decision to leave the Marines in pursuit of the American Dream.

Optimism buoyed him as he transitioned to civilian life, drawn by the promise of a larger paycheck. However, reality soon set in as the economy took a nosedive shortly after he departed from the military. The job market tightened, and opportunities dwindled.

John's hopes were dashed when he lost his job as a computer technician—a role he had hoped would provide stability and advancement. With bills mounting and a family to support, he reluctantly accepted a position at a dry-cleaning plant, earning minimum wage.

The transition from military to civilian life proved to be more challenging than John had thought.

John's days were consumed by the persistent struggle to keep his head above water. His financial burdens bore down on him like a suffocating blanket, leaving him gasping for air. With bills piling up like an insurmountable mountain and the constant threat of home foreclosure looming overhead, John knew he needed to take drastic action. It was during a fleeting moment of respite, a brief interlude during the grind of his daily routine, that John made his decision. He sat on a bench outside the dry-cleaning plant. It was break time, and his thoughts drifted back to the conversation he had with his colleague Ben when he worked as a computer technician.

"Hey, John, you seem stressed. Everything okay?" Ben noticed.

"Yeah, just trying to juggle all these bills." John shrugged as a matter of fact and sat on his chair with a loud sigh.

"I hear you, man. Did you ever consider filing for Chapter 7 bankruptcy?" Ben asked.

John's brow furrowed in confusion. The term was familiar to him, but he was not aware of the details. "Chapter 7 bankruptcy? What's that?" John looked at him.

His colleague leaned in, "It's a way to get a fresh start, financially speaking. You sell off nonexempt possessions to repay your creditors, but you get to keep certain exempt assets. Once it's all said and done, the remaining debts are discharged."

John's eyes widened as his colleague's words sunk in. Could this be the solution he had been searching for?

"Here's the attorney's contact who helped me through the process." He handed John the card.

"That sounds... promising. Thanks for the tip; I'll look into it." John thanked him with a smile, took the card, and slid it into his pants pocket. But during the daily grind, he forgot to even look at it. The prospect had slipped his mind until now. John mulled over his colleague's advice, and a solution welled up within him. He quickly pulled out the card from his pants and carefully examined it, tracing his finger over the embossed letters of Attorney Keith Rodger's name. With a deep breath, he decided to take the leap and seek professional guidance. This was his chance to take control of his financial destiny and carve out a path toward a brighter future for himself and his family.

Dialing the number listed on the card, John anxiously waited as the phone rang. Finally, a soft, feminine voice answered on the other end. "Good afternoon, Law Offices. How may I assist you?"

Clearing his throat, John replied, "Yes, I'd like to inquire about booking an appointment with Attorney Keith Rodgers, please."

"Certainly, sir. Let me check his availability for you," the receptionist replied politely before putting John on hold momentarily.

After a brief wait, she returned to the line. "Mr. Rodgers has an opening tomorrow morning at 10:00 a.m. Will that work for you?"

Relieved, John confirmed the appointment and thanked the receptionist before hanging up. The next day, he called in sick to work, knowing that this was an important step toward resolving his financial troubles. As he drove to Attorney Keith's office, John couldn't shake off the nerves that fluttered in his stomach. Arriving at the address mentioned on the card, he stepped into the sleek, professional atmosphere of the law firm's lobby.

Moments later, he was ushered into Attorney Keith's office. The attorney stood to greet him, his warm smile putting John at ease.

"Good morning, I'm Keith Rodgers. Please, have a seat," Keith gestured toward a comfortable leather chair opposite his desk.

"John Aaden," he said and took the seat, clearing his throat. Here was someone who was going to help him with his financial troubles.

"How can I assist you today, Mr. Aaden?" Keith asked.

John took a deep breath, steeling himself for the conversation, "I'm here to file for Chapter 7 bankruptcy."

"Why?" Keith's question was direct yet devoid of judgment, allowing John the space to share his story. And share, he did. John recounted his journey, from his early career choices to the current financial predicament that hovered over him like a cloud.

When John finished speaking, Keith's response was reassuring. "Given your circumstances, Chapter 7 bankruptcy indeed seems appropriate."

Relief flooded through John as he absorbed Keith's words.

"Allow me to explain the eligibility criteria for Chapter 7 bankruptcy," Keith prepared to explain the details, "To qualify for relief under Chapter 7 of the Bankruptcy Code, the debtor may be an individual, a partnership, or a corporation or other business entity. Subject to the means test described above for individual debtors, relief is available under Chapter 7 irrespective of the amount of the debtor's debts or whether the debtor is solvent or insolvent."

John listened intently, absorbing every word as Keith continued, "However, it's important to note that an individual cannot file under Chapter 7 or any other chapter if, during the preceding 180 days, a prior bankruptcy petition was dismissed due to the debtor's willful failure to appear before the court or comply with orders of the court, or the debtor voluntarily dismissed the previous case after creditors sought relief from the bankruptcy court to recover property upon which they hold liens."

John nodded. This was his chance for a fresh start - a chance to unburden himself from his debts and begin anew.

Keith said, "One of the primary purposes of bankruptcy is to discharge certain debts to give an honest individual debtor a 'fresh start.' The debtor has no liability for discharged debts. In a Chapter 7 case, however, a discharge is only available to individual debtors, not to partnerships or corporations. Although an individual Chapter 7 case usually results in a discharge of debts, the right to a discharge is not absolute, and some types of debts are not discharged. Moreover, a bankruptcy discharge does not extinguish a lien on the property."

As Keith concluded his explanation, John felt resolved to go for it. It was the only option now. The road ahead would be fraught with challenges, but for the first time in what felt like an eternity, he dared to hope for a brighter future.

John sat at his desk, surrounded by paperwork, as he began the process of filing for Chapter 7 bankruptcy. With a furrowed brow, he carefully filled out the official bankruptcy forms, ensuring every detail was accurate. As he completed the forms, he compiled a list of all his creditors and their claims, noting down the amount and nature of each debt. His income, expenses, and property were documented, leaving no stone unturned.

"Alright, let's see... creditors, income, expenses," John muttered to himself, checking off every item on the list. With all the paperwork in order, he handed over the documents, expecting to pay the required fees. However, to his relief, Keith informed him that his fees would be waived due to his income falling below the defined poverty level, but some service charges couldn't be excluded, which were about $1200 in total.

"Thank you," John breathed a sigh of relief. That was mostly all he had for now.

Weeks passed, and John took a day off to go to the San Diego Central Courthouse for his case. Exiting onto Front Street from the Civic Center, he felt grit course through his mind. The streets of downtown San Diego teemed with life. Turning right onto West B Street, John drove on, hoping to find reprieve from the onslaught of his financial woes.

As he reached the intersection of West B Street and Union Street, John's gaze fell upon the formidable structure of the San Diego Central Courthouse. Its imposing façade stood before him like a fortress of justice.

With a deep breath, John stepped into the courthouse, his footsteps tapping softly on the sleek, polished wooden floors. As he walked through the minimalist corridors, John felt trepidation stir in him. Finally, he reached the designated hall. The air was crisp and clean, with a hint of citrus from the freshly brewed coffee nearby. Taking his seat, he awaited his turn. Soon, he stood before the judge. The atmosphere was tense as the judge reviewed his case.

"Mr. Aaden, after reviewing your petition and considering the circumstances, I hereby grant your bankruptcy discharge," the judge announced. This was his first bankruptcy, and he was glad that everything went without much hassle.

"Thank you, Your Honor," John replied and left the courtroom. He was positive that now he would be able to restart his life. But just as one burden seemed to lift, another flooded his life. A few days later, John received the unexpected news that his wife had filed for divorce. The initial shock left him reeling. His mind struggled to comprehend the sudden turn of events. How could this be happening? Hadn't they weathered countless storms together? It wasn't as if the idea of divorce hadn't been broached before; there had been signs – subtle hints of discontent, fleeting moments of tension that had gone unaddressed. But John hadn't taken those warning signs seriously, clinging to the hope that they could weather any storm together.

John confronted his wife as his heart sank. The reality of their situation sank in. He had been so consumed by his own struggles that he had failed to see the cracks forming in their marriage. And now, faced with the harsh truth, he realized just how far they had drifted apart.

Sitting across from Chandice, John felt his heart heavy with sorrow and regret. The tension in the room was evident as they faced each other. Only now were the unresolved concerns rising to the surface like a dead body.

"Chandice, I don't understand," John began, "We've been through so much together. Why now?"

Chandice met his gaze. "John, it's been over a decade, and we're still at zero. No progress. Nothing," she replied, "I can't keep living like this. I need to move on."

John felt a lump form in his throat as her words hit him like a punch to the gut. He wanted to protest, to plead with her to give their marriage another chance. But deep down, he knew she was right. They had been stuck in a cycle of discontent for far too long.

"But what about us? What about our family?" John pleaded.

Chandice shook her head sadly, "I'm sorry, John. But I can't keep waiting for things to change."

The reality of their impending divorce sank in. John's heart felt like it was breaking into a million pieces. He never imagined his life would end up like this – alone, broke, and facing yet another court battle in a year's time. With a heavy sigh, he nodded silently, knowing that fighting would only prolong the inevitable. "Okay, Chandice. I understand," he whispered and left.

Four months later, the divorce proceedings were finalized. He felt traumatized by the abrupt end of his marriage and the unraveling of his life. John felt as though his world had been shattered into a million irreparable pieces. Each day felt like a struggle to simply get out of bed and face the harsh reality of his new circumstances. The children, who were now 10 and 11 years old, were living with Chandice, and he agreed to pay child support. His financial situation was already strained to the breaking point.

Sitting alone in his empty room, John reflected on the twists and turns his life had taken. At 35 years old, he felt like he had hit rock bottom – his dreams shattered, his future uncertain, and his bank account empty. This wasn't the life he had hoped for himself.

Despite clinging to his minimum-paying job as a lifeline, John found himself retreating further and further into a shell of semi-isolation. The vibrant aspects of his life – his church community, his friends, even his children – now felt like distant memories, lost in the shadow of his despair.

Days turned into weeks, and weeks turned into months, as John struggled with the overwhelming depression. He became a ghost of his former self, avoiding social gatherings and main events with a sense of numb resignation. Instead, he sat in solitude of his thoughts, endlessly replaying moments from his past life and the haunting question of what to do next. In the quiet moments of reflection, John came to a sobering realization – that perhaps some of his own decisions had led him to this bleak juncture. Despite his well-managed efforts and planning, he was at a loss when it came to his finances. Despite his best intentions, he couldn't seem to make any headway, and the reasons behind his financial stagnation remained frustratingly vague.

To John, the American Dream was not just a vague concept; it was a well-crafted vision - a personalized blueprint for the life he aspired to lead. It encompassed far more than mere material wealth. The American Dream meant the freedom to carve out his path, to dictate his chosen lifestyle without constraint or limitation. It embodied the ideals of self-directedness, self-sufficiency, and self-reliance – the ability to chart his course through life's unforgiving waters with autonomy.

For John, the pursuit of happiness was not just a lofty ideal of becoming a millionaire; it was a quest for a state of well-being and contentment. It meant having enough financial stability to travel where he pleased, buy what he needed, and pursue his passions without worrying about the cost of goods or incurring debt.

However, as John observed the reality of many people's lives, including his own brother Nathan's, he felt disillusioned. For far too many, the American Dream had been reduced to a hollow shell – a life shackled by debt, consumed by the pursuit of material possessions, and trapped in a never-ending cycle of paycheck-to-paycheck existence - the one he was enduring now. This wasn't the life he desired. John pondered if this was what many people now consider to be the American Dream. If this is the case, he was not impressed.

The image of luxury cars with burdensome loan payments, stacks of credit cards used to bridge financial gaps, and sleepless nights haunted by pending debt balances painted a bleak portrait of modern-day slavery. It was a life dictated by lienholders, creditors, bosses, supervisors, banks, the IRS, and other government agencies. As a result, most individuals work 40-50 hours per week, get home exhausted, shop with credit cards because they are cash-strapped, fret about the debt they accumulate, spend their whole paycheck on bills and debt, and repeat the cycle year after year until death. John, too, felt stuck in the same system and desired to escape. He did not want a life where individuals toiled tirelessly only to find themselves perpetually ensnared in the trappings of consumerism and financial dependency. He yearned for more – for a life of abundance, security, and genuine wealth. He wanted to break free from the suffocating grip of financial servitude and step into true prosperity.

But how? What separated the wealthy from the impoverished, the successful from the struggling? These questions gnawed at John's conscience, fueling his pursuit for answers. He longed to find the formula that would elevate him from rags to riches, from obscurity to success.

"Is there such a thing? A formula to riches?" he muttered to himself, "There must be, and I need to find it."

CHAPTER 5

❧

Starting from the Bottom

One year after emerging from a dark cloud of depression, John decided it was time to take control of his life again. He felt a stirring within him, a hunger for knowledge and a drive to pursue his dreams. He now set his sights on education, seeing it as a pathway to a brighter future – the American dream.

Enrolling at the University of San Diego at the age of 36 began a steady six-year journey for John. As a non-traditional student returning to academia after many years, John faced unique challenges and opportunities. To finance his education, John applied for a student loan to cover the cost of his initial class enrollment. Even though he worked during the day, this financial assistance was important as he had no other means to pay the substantial tuition fees.

John came to know about psychology in his first year of high school. From the moment he encountered the subject, he was captivated by its depth. As of now, after more than a decade, John's decision to pursue a degree in psychology was driven by two compelling reasons.

First and foremost, John recognized the importance of understanding himself better, especially in light of his recent battle with depression. Emerging from the darkness of mental illness, he yearned for clarity and insight into his own psyche. Psychology, with its focus on human behavior and mental processes, offered him a pathway to self-discovery and healing. Alongside his personal growth, John ignored the practical considerations that fueled his decision. The prospect of financial stability played a significant role in his choice to pursue psychology as a career. Aware of the lucrative opportunities available to psychologists, particularly those who catered to an affluent clientele, John saw the potential for a comfortable lifestyle and financial independence. While his passion for the field was genuine, he also saw it as a means to secure his future and achieve financial security.

He stepped inside the classroom, buzzing with the conversations of young pupils. John felt he was the only older one, but that was not a problem. Learning should not have any age. John sat at his desk, and just then, the professor entered. John's gaze was now fixed on the front of the room where the professor stood, ready for the class on the neurological basis of behavior.

Students flipped open their notebooks and adjusted their pens. The professor began the lecture. "Today, we will explore the neurological mechanisms that underpin human behavior," she announced, "From the firing of neurons to the complex interaction of neurotransmitters, we will explore how the brain shapes our thoughts, emotions, and actions."

As the professor launched into her explanation, John found himself captivated by the concept of neurons and synapses described before him. With each slide projected onto the screen, he scribbled furiously in his notebook, trying to capture every detail. The professor's knowledge of the subject was vast, and John felt eager to learn.

"Let's start by discussing the role of neurotransmitters in regulating mood and behavior," the professor continued, gesturing to a diagram displayed on the screen. "From dopamine to serotonin, these chemical messengers play an important role in shaping our emotional experiences and influencing our actions."

As the lecture progressed, John found himself engrossed in the complexities of the brain's reward system, neurotransmitter pathways, and the influence of genetics on behavior. The professor's explanations were clear and concise, challenging John to think critically and engage with the material on a deeper level.

The professor paused, allowing for questions and discussion. John seized the opportunity and raised his hand, inquiring, "Professor, how does everyone's differences in brain structure and function contribute to variations in behavior?"

The professor nodded approvingly, impressed by John's insightful question. "Ah, an excellent point," she replied, "Variations in brain structure, such as differences in cortical thickness or neural connectivity, can influence everything from personality traits to cognitive abilities."

The classroom came alive as the discussion went on. All the students started sharing their perspectives and insights. As the lecture drew to a close, John felt a sense of exhilaration. He couldn't wait to explore the mysteries of the brain further, both inside and outside the classroom. The second class of the evening had ended. John glanced at his watch and felt a pang of relief. He had to hurry home now to catch some rest before another full day of work. Balancing his studies with a full-time job was tough but necessary.

John gathered his belongings and hurried out of the classroom. The transition from the vibrant campus to the tranquility of the night was a brief respite before the next day's demands. However, with time, John became accustomed to this juggling act, mastering the balance between work and studies.

Months turned into years as John's routine of working during the day and attending evening and night classes continued. Despite the constant demands on his time and energy, John's dedication to both his education and his job never withered.

Now, as he made his way to his evening class after work, John reflected on his college experience - online lectures and brick-and-mortar classes. Some days, it felt like a marathon with no end in sight. There were moments when he wanted to throw in the towel, to give up on his dreams of earning a degree. Tough subjects, demanding research papers, and impending school deadlines overwhelmed him sometimes.

But despite the challenges, John persisted. He reminded himself of the bigger picture, of the dreams and aspirations driving him forward. Quitting was not an option, not when he had come this far. So, with determination in his heart, John pushed through the tough times, knowing that every obstacle he overcame brought him a step closer to his goals. As he headed to work once again, John carried with him the resilience and perseverance that defined his college journey. The road ahead might be long and arduous, but he was ready to face whatever challenges came his way. After all, quitting was never in his vocabulary—success was.

One of the most rewarding aspects of studying psychology was the opportunity to conduct practical, human-based research. John relished the chance to apply theoretical concepts to real-world scenarios, tangibly testing his understanding. The interactions during these practical sessions, whether with juniors or classmates, were experiences that added to his learning.

During his internship as a counselor in a school for adolescents, John gained invaluable insights into human behavior. Getting to know people on a deeper level, beyond superficial interactions, opened his mind to the complexities of the human psyche. It was an experience he couldn't imagine having in any other field of study.

As a voracious reader, John found joy in exploring the vast literature of psychology. From reference books to scholarly articles, the subject was so engrossing and relevant that even 'textbooks' felt like novels.

Preparing for examinations definitely posed its challenges, particularly the balance between theory and practical application. John wished for more guidance on adapting his knowledge to essay-type answers and for a more relaxed approach to practical exams. Reflecting on his own experiences, he recognized the importance of making the subject more student-friendly without compromising on its quality.

And so, after four years of undergraduate studies and two years of a rigorous master's degree program, John emerged victorious. At the age of 42, he held in his hands the academic credentials that would pave the way for his future. But as he looked up, his heart swelled with even greater joy, for beside him stood his beloved Kate Rice.

Their relationship had begun in the halls of academia, where fate had brought them together during John's graduate program. Kate was a business major, and she was doing her MBA. With her sharp intellect and easy charm, she had captured John's attention from the moment they first met. Their friendship blossomed quickly into something more. From candlelit dinners at cozy restaurants to leisurely strolls through parks, each moment spent together felt like a valued memory in the making. They laughed, they talked, and they dreamed of a future with endless possibilities.

One particularly memorable evening, John surprised Kate with tickets to a live concert by her favorite band, Heart. The excitement filled her as they entered the venue, surrounded by a crowd of enthusiastic fans. 'Heart' was known for its powerful blend of hard rock, but its music spanned across multiple genres, from folk to pop, and even touches of heavy metal. As the concert began, the stage lights dimmed, and the band members took their places. The electric energy of the guitars, the deep thrum of the bass, and the thunderous beat of the drums filled their surroundings, creating an atmosphere. Ann Wilson's voice soared through the venue, strong and clear, as they began singing "Dreamboat Annie." The song's gentle acoustic opening gradually built into a more intense, rock-driven melody, showcasing the band's versatility.

Kate was captivated by the performance. The way Heart combined soulful lyrics with powerful instrumentation demonstrated that rock wasn't just a man's game—these women could rock just as hard. The harmony of Ann and Nancy Wilson's voices, the intricate guitar solos, and the driving rhythm section created a sound that was both nostalgic and fresh. Kate loved every moment, singing along to every song and feeling inspired by the strength.

As the music filled their ears and the crowd swayed to the rhythm, John stole glances at the beautiful smile lighting up Kate's face. In that moment, surrounded by the pulsating energy of the crowd, they felt a connection that only grew stronger with each passing day.

During their romantic escapades, John and Kate also found time to discuss their plans for the future. One crisp autumn evening, as they strolled hand in hand through a picturesque park ablaze with golden foliage, John mused, "I would like a place where every room is decked with luxurious furniture and grandeur, a true refuge where we may create a life of love and laughter."

Kate's eyes sparkled as she continued, "And a garden with purple tulips if we are dreaming. We could spend lazy afternoons sipping tea on the porch, watching the sunset paint the sky with hues of pink and orange."

"That's a very romantic portrayal for an MBA student," John remarked, eliciting a chuckle from Kate.

"You mean MBAs can't be romantic? How dare you," she teased.

Their banter continued, and in between, they discussed everything from the color of the walls to the layout of the kitchen. But their dreams didn't end there. Fuelled by their shared ambition and entrepreneurial spirit, John and Kate also explored the possibility of starting their own business ventures. Over cups of steaming coffee at their favorite café, they brainstormed ideas, bouncing concepts off each other.

"I've been thinking about our future, and I had this idea of starting our own business," John shared.

"Oh really? What's the idea?" Kate leaned forward.

"I was thinking about getting into real estate. With the housing market booming, I think it could be a lucrative venture." John sipped on his coffee.

"Hmm, that's an interesting idea, John. But have you considered pet sitting as a business opportunity? I have always thought about it," Kate suggested.

"Pet sitting? I hadn't thought about that."

"Well, did you know that about 70% of US families have pets? And when these families go away for extended periods, they need someone they can trust to take care of their furry friends. That's where pet sitting comes in," Kate shared with pride.

"I see. So, what exactly does pet sitting involve?" John asked with curiosity.

"As pet sitters, we would watch over our clients' dogs, cats, or other pets at their house. We'd need to feed them, give them water, play with them, and take dogs for walks as needed. It's all about providing peace of mind to pet owners while they're away."

"That sounds like a rewarding job. And you mentioned something about running two income streams simultaneously?" John said.

"Exactly. If we have other sources of income that only require an internet connection and a laptop, like freelance work or online businesses, we can work on those while pet sitting. Most pet owners would be happy to let us work on our laptops while we're taking care of their pets." Kate replied, smiling.

John's eyes sparkled, "Wow, Kate, I'm impressed. Pet sitting seems like a great business idea, especially considering the growing number of pet owners. Let's explore this further and see if we can turn it into a successful venture."

During all their dreams and aspirations, there was one thing they both agreed on—children were not part of their plans. Instead, John focused his energy on supporting the children from his first marriage, ensuring they had the resources and guidance needed to pursue their own dreams.

After two years, at the age of 44, John and Kate tied the knot of matrimony, embracing the first step of their dreams. As they stood hand in hand, gazing out at the horizon of countless possibilities, John and Kate knew that their love would only continue to grow stronger with each passing year.

CHAPTER 6

❧

A Way Up

With renewed motivation, a supportive wife, and a master's degree in psychology, John began to see a brighter future. He intended to help students deal with their personal and academic challenges. Shortly after graduation, John started working with Riverside, California High School District, conducting advanced assessment and counseling sessions with students. His days were filled with meaningful interactions, offering guidance, listening to their struggles, and celebrating their triumphs. The sense of fulfillment he gained from his work was immense, but the dream of owning a business never left him.

His wife, Kate, was an ambitious and creative spirit. She wanted to be self-employed, which was okay with him. John always liked the idea of having his own business, and this was the chance to do it.

John and Kate often spent their evenings discussing their dreams and aspirations on the back porch of their cozy home in Riverside, the scent of blooming jasmine wafting through the warm California breeze.

One evening, as the sun dipped below the horizon and the sky painted itself in hues of orange and pink,

Kate leaned forward, "John, I've been thinking a lot about our future business. What if we opened a wellness center? A place where people can come to get counseling, take part in workshops, and even do some creative arts therapy?"

John's eyes lit up at the idea. "That's brilliant, Kate. We could combine our skills—my background in psychology and your business and creative talents. We could really make a difference in people's lives."

Kate smiled, "Exactly! We could offer personalized therapy sessions, group workshops, art classes, and even mindfulness and relaxation techniques. It could be a holistic approach to mental and emotional well-being."

"I love it," John said, leaning back in his chair and picturing their dream coming to life, "And we could create a welcoming environment, one that feels safe and nurturing. A place where people feel supported and understood."

They spent the next few weeks sketching out their business plan called 'Harmony Wellness.' Their dining table was soon covered in notebooks, sketches, and brochures from other wellness centers. Every free moment was spent brainstorming and researching. Kate was the creative force, designing logos and drafting ideas for workshop themes. John focused on the practical aspects, looking into licenses, potential locations, and the best ways to incorporate their services.

After much research, they realized the idea of the wellness center required a massive investment, more than what they could afford or borrowed at the beginning. Six months after getting married, they were invited to join a promising multilevel business opportunity called "Evergreen Enterprises." The company sold eco-friendly home products and emphasized sustainable living, which aligned well with their values. One evening, they attended a presentation at a local hotel. The room hummed with excitement as the speaker, a charismatic man named Robert, explained the company's vision and the potential for financial freedom. "At Evergreen Enterprises, we're not just selling products," Robert enthused. "We're promoting a lifestyle. Imagine working for yourself, setting your own hours, and making a difference in the world."

The numbers looked good, the work was doable, and the time commitment was feasible. John and Kate exchanged hopeful glances. "This could be our chance to save enough for Harmony Wellness," Kate whispered.

So, they halted their own business idea and dove into Evergreen Enterprises. They attended training sessions, networked persistently, and registered a few people under them. Their garage was soon filled with boxes of bamboo kitchenware, organic cleaning supplies, and energy-efficient light bulbs.

At first, it seemed promising. They hosted parties, gave product demonstrations, and even converted their friends and family into loyal customers.

However, as the months passed, they struggled to build the momentum needed to expand the business on a larger scale. Recruitment was tough, and their downline didn't grow as anticipated. One year later, they were still at ground zero, barely breaking even. Disheartened but not defeated, they decided to cut their losses and leave Evergreen Enterprises. "We gave it our best shot," John said, squeezing Kate's hand. "It's time to move on."

They then turned their attention to real estate, hoping to capitalize on the booming market. Kate got a real estate brokerage license, and John obtained a real estate agent license. Together, they opened a real estate business called "Riverside Realty." They employed a couple more agents, and business started booming. For a good year and a half, they generated steady business revenue and paid themselves good salaries. Initially, things looked promising as they helped a few clients find their dream homes, but soon after, the housing market in California took a nosedive because of high interest rates. Revenue came to a dead stop as people stopped buying houses. Their income dwindled, and the expenses of running the business piled up. At this point, they were surviving mostly on John's income from his full-time commitment to the school, which was not enough to sustain their lifestyle.

Kate sighed one evening as they reviewed their finances. 'This market is brutal, John. We're barely keeping our heads above water."

"I know," John replied with frustration evident in his voice, "Maybe it's time to rethink our strategy."

Next, they invested in a floral franchise business called "Petal Pioneers." The idea was to bring joy to people through beautiful, sustainable floral arrangements. Business was steady at first, with a regular flow of customers for weddings, events, and everyday floral needs. However, franchise fees and regular expenses ate into their profits, leaving them with little to show for their hard work.

Two years into the venture, it became clear that the floral business wasn't going to provide the financial security they needed. "We're stuck, Kate," John said, running a hand through his hair. "The revenue isn't enough, and the future looks bleak."

With heavy hearts, they sold the franchise and left the floral business altogether. After five years of being involved in business with little success, John and Kate decided to bring all their business ventures to a halt. Despite their entrepreneurial spirit, their financial situation had become precarious.

By then, they had moved to an exclusive neighborhood in California, purchased a new, sprawling home with a picturesque view, and financed two luxury cars, a sleek black Mercedes and a Sepang bronze metallic BMW – all during their period of substantial financial success, i.e., real estate venture. Confident in their continued success, they accumulated a large amount of debt, including a hefty mortgage, adding to their significant student loans, personal loans, and mounting credit card debt.

From a distance, John and Kate appeared successful. They both held advanced college degrees, lived in an attractive neighborhood, and drove expensive cars. Their life looked like a picture of success, yet behind closed doors, the reality was starkly different. Financial instability hovered over them like a constant cloud, with minimal cash reserves and deep, suffocating debt. One evening, as they sat in their tastefully decorated living room, Kate broke the silence that had been growing between them. "John, I've been thinking a lot," she began, "This... this isn't working. The constant stress, the financial strain... it's too much. I feel like I'm drowning."

John looked up from his laptop, "Kate, I know things have been tough, but we can get through this." For a moment, he felt like he had plummeted into a similar situation to his past when Chandice said the same words. Panic gripped his heart. Is his life going in a circle?

Kate shook her head as tears welled up in her eyes. "It's not just about the money, John. I feel like we've lost ourselves, lost each other. I need to find myself again, and I think I'd be better off alone."

The words hit John like a punch to the gut. He took a deep breath, trying to process what she was saying. "Are you asking for a divorce?" he asked quietly, his voice barely above a whisper.

Kate nodded, "I'm so sorry, John. I never wanted it to come to this. But I can't keep living like this. I need to start over."

John's heart sank. He had known things were bad, but he hadn't realized just how far apart they had grown. "If that's what you really want, Kate, I won't stand in your way. I love you, and I want you to be happy, even if that means being apart."

At 49 years old, roughly six years after his first family tragedy, John found himself at a crossroads. Despite having a stable job as a counselor at Riverside High School, the prospect of a looming divorce, a high mortgage payment, car loans, student loans, credit card debt, and personal loans made his head spin. The financial burden seemed insurmountable. Even if the responsibility were to be split in half, it would take him years to repay his portion.

He had tried everything to save his marriage. Long, heartfelt conversations with Kate, couples counseling sessions, and attempts to rekindle their romance had all fallen short. Kate eventually filed for divorce, citing irreconcilable differences. The process was emotionally draining, and the financial toll was heavy.

The next few weeks were a blur of painful conversations and difficult decisions. They sold their dream home at a loss and downsized to separate apartments. The luxury cars were returned and replaced with more practical, used vehicles. They negotiated debt balances and went their separate ways. John took on extra work, offering private counseling sessions and tutoring to make ends meet.

Now, with no savings or investments and just enough income from his job to cover rent and basic survival needs, John found himself at a daunting financial crossroads. His debt was overwhelming: $150,000 in student loans, $45,000 in credit card debt, and $50,000 in personal loans. Even after a few months of working in a retail facility on the weekends, John's body could hardly sustain the grueling demand his debt had placed on him. The physical strain of long hours on his feet, combined with the emotional toll of his financial struggles, left him feeling utterly exhausted.

One evening, as he collapsed onto his worn-out couch, his phone buzzed with a message from his old friend from the University of San Diego, Mike. "Hey, John. Haven't heard from you in a while. How's everything going?"

John sighed and typed a response. "Not great, Mike. I'm struggling. Need to talk."

Within minutes, his phone rang. Mike's voice was a comforting reminder of better days. "John, you've always been one of the toughest people I know. But it sounds like you're really going through it. What's going on?"

John hesitated, then poured his heart out. "Mike, I'm drowning in debt. I've been working myself to the bone, but it's not enough. I've been thinking about filing for bankruptcy again, but it feels like admitting defeat."

Mike listened patiently and then offered some advice. "John, you've got to take care of yourself first. Filing for bankruptcy doesn't make you a failure. It's a tool to help you reset. Maybe it's time to focus on getting back on your feet without killing yourself in the process."

After months of mulling over his personal and financial issues and talking with a few trusted friends and family members, John finally made the difficult decision. He filed for Chapter 7 bankruptcy again in Hemet, California. Even though he felt relieved that he was discharged, John still felt the burden of his circumstances. His way of life was now developing into a steady pattern of undeniable failures that troubled him deeply. Repeated divorces, heavy spending, large debt balances, no savings, no investments, bankruptcies, and feeling emotionally trapped had left him questioning everything.

John wondered what he was doing so wrong that kept him trapped in this cycle. He had thought more education, a higher-paying job, and a better career would solve these financial problems. Somehow, this typical mantra of the streets wasn't working for him. Instead, he found himself no better off financially than when he first arrived in the country. Apart from his academic credentials, he hadn't moved up. Thank goodness for the bankruptcy courts that kept him from total financial ruination.

One night, as he sat in his modest apartment, surrounded by the remnants of his past ventures, he thought about his brother Nathan. Nathan had settled into a quiet life, accepting his fate and finding contentment in simplicity. John wondered if that was the path he should take. Should he coast the rest of the way toward the end of his life, like most people, until death?

Deep inside, something burned within him that he couldn't ignore. The passion for financial independence still blazed, even if it was a small flame amid the darkness. He refused to accept the idea of being a loser. Although he had no idea how he would change his current circumstances, he was quietly hoping to run into a solution that would catapult him into a better financial situation.

Maybe it wasn't too late for him.

The road ahead was uncertain, but for the first time in a long while, he felt a glimmer of hope that his story could still have a better ending.

CHAPTER 7

❧

An Angel In Disguise

John always believed that life is unfair. He often reflected on how some people were born into wealth, basking in the luxury of generational fortunes, while others toiled endlessly just to make ends meet, and still, some remain ensnared in the relentless grip of poverty with no escape in sight. It's been that way since the dawn of human existence, he thought, and it will never change. His option was the middle one, and he knew it. He had never been deluded into thinking that fate would be kinder to him than to anyone else.

But to this point, he had done the best he knew how. In his quieter moments, he admitted his mistakes to himself, acknowledging the times he had stumbled or made poor decisions. He had served his country in the military, a chapter of his life that filled him with pride. He had pursued higher education and fought his way through countless sleepless nights and financial hurdles to earn his degree. He had embarked on a promising career and built and lost several businesses.

Each failure was stamped into his memory with an ungodly amount of money and effort expended trying to get ahead. Yet, despite these efforts, he was nowhere closer to his dream 30 years later than when he started in his early twenties. John knew he wasn't naive about the role of money in his life. He pondered this often, turning it over in his mind like a well-worn coin. He didn't believe that money answered all the problems. He valued the intangible things—relationships with friends and family, the warmth of human connection—far more than he valued money. However, he couldn't ignore the undeniable fact that money played a significant role in people's lives. With cash, a person could pay monthly bills without a second thought, eliminate the crushing weight of debt, send a child to college without the specter of loans looming overhead, put money down on a valuable purchase without the anxiety of financial strain, build an emergency reserve for those inevitable rainy days, generate various income streams, and set oneself free financially.

He often ruminated on the additional benefits money brought and the subtle yet important ways it influenced one's status in the community. Those with a lot of it commanded more respect, experienced more security, exhibited tremendous control and power, and enjoyed an extraordinary degree of personal freedom. John's thoughts would darken as he considered the flip side of this coin. Life without money could be harsh and unforgiving.

Those with little or none of it struggled to pay their rent or mortgage, buy food, or fix essential things that broke down. These financial hardships often translated into a cascade of adverse conditions: homelessness, hunger, isolation, poor health, and a myriad of other struggles that gnawed at one's soul. As far as John was concerned, he was perilously close to these adverse conditions. The only thing keeping him from utter financial chaos was his current job. It was a lifeline that held his life together. Despite his personal and financial setbacks, a stubborn spark of hope remained within him. He believed things would improve. He had to. Now, more than ever, he was even more gritty about changing his circumstances, though he was still unsure how to proceed from here.

Sitting in his small, cluttered room late one night, John stared at the stacks of documents and bills that seemed to mock his efforts. He rubbed his temples, feeling the familiar tension building. "What's next?" he muttered to himself, the words barely audible in the stillness. His mind raced with possibilities and dead ends. He knew he needed a new plan, a new approach. Something different from the countless attempts that had left him standing in the same place, year after year. The uncertainty pressed down on him, but he forced himself to stand, squaring his shoulders against the invisible burden.

"Tomorrow is another day," he told himself. And with that, he turned off the light, plunging the room into darkness.

***

The next day, John had registered himself to attend the "Pathways to Prosperity" business seminar in Anaheim, California, hoping to find a way forward. The seminar was highly anticipated, drawing entrepreneurs and business enthusiasts from all over the state. The venue whirred with energy as attendees mingled, exchanged business cards, and networked with like-minded individuals.

John walked through the crowd, looking for the missing piece to his financial puzzle. The large conference hall was filled with booths showcasing different aspects of business success, from investment strategies to innovative technologies.

John decided to attend a session on entrepreneurial resilience, taking a seat near the front. The speaker, a well-known business coach, delivered an inspiring talk on overcoming setbacks and seizing opportunities. John's mind flowed with new ideas and possibilities. During the Q&A session, John asked a question about sustaining motivation during difficult times, earning a nod of approval from the speaker.

After the session, John wandered through the exhibit area, stopping occasionally to chat with other attendees and presenters. It was at one of these booths, displaying a new financial management software, that he met Matthew Bell. Matthew was a 51-year-old Caucasian man with a confident demeanor and a warm smile. His presence was both commanding and approachable.

"Hi there. Are you interested in financial management?" Matthew asked, noticing John's curiosity.

"Yes, absolutely," John replied.

Matthew extended his hand, "Matthew Bell. Nice to meet you."

"John. Nice to meet you too," John responded, shaking his hand firmly.

They struck up a conversation, and John quickly learned that Matthew was a self-made millionaire from La Jolla, California. Matthew shared snippets of his journey from humble beginnings to financial success, and John found himself captivated by his story.

"What brought you to this seminar?" Matthew asked, noting the pamphlet in John's hand.

"I'm hoping to find some guidance on how to get ahead financially," John admitted. "I've tried so many things, but I feel like I'm stuck in the same place."

Matthew nodded, "I've been there. It's not easy to break through those barriers, but it's possible."

They continued talking, sharing their thoughts on economics, business strategies, and personal challenges. There was a genuine connection between them, a shared understanding of the struggles and aspirations that come with pursuing financial independence.

Before parting ways, they exchanged contact information. "Let's meet again," Matthew suggested. "I'd love to continue our conversation. Maybe over coffee?"

"That sounds great," John replied, feeling a surge of hope. "I'd really appreciate your insights."

They promised to meet again later, and as John left the seminar, he felt a renewed sense of optimism. Meeting Matthew felt like a turning point, a ray of light in the dark cave of his financial instability.

One sunny afternoon, as they sat in Caroline's Seaside Cafe in La Jolla, John couldn't contain his excitement about the prospect of their friendship. He felt that Matthew was an angel from heaven, one with answers to all his questions about the American Dream, business, money, wealth, getting ahead, and becoming a millionaire.

During their first meeting, John raised some hypothetical questions, hoping Matthew would address them in the many sessions ahead. With a notebook open in front of him, John began, "America is one of the world's most affluent countries, right? So why is it so hard to make ends meet, let alone get ahead in this country?"

Matthew leaned back, listening intently as John continued, "The more I spend, the more debt I accumulate. Is that truly how it is with most people? Would you say most of the people in this country are broke? How do I break away from the paycheck-to-paycheck cycle permanently? What must I do to get ahead and stay ahead financially? Is it truly possible to go from rags to riches in this country? Can I become a millionaire like you?"

Matthew wasn't entirely surprised by these initial questions—they were common among those seeking financial wisdom. However, like a good mentor, he promised to address each and a few more during their sessions titled 'Wealth Building' sessions – 'The Way to the Top in America.'

"John, as you may have come to realize," Matthew began, "achieving financial independence isn't easy. It requires more than simply obtaining a college degree, getting a good job, and working hard. There are too many people in the world who are well-educated and hard-working but still broke."

Matthew's expression grew more serious as he continued, "Unless you win the lottery or inherit a sum of money, pulling yourself from the bottom to the top financially will be the hardest thing you will ever do. It is so because most people ignore some basic money management concepts or simply don't know how to go about the process."

He paused, letting his words sink in before adding, "During our meetings, I'll show you where most people go wrong with their finances and how to avoid these pitfalls for success. But before unraveling these situations, let me show you where most people 'are' financially. It will take us a couple of sessions to cover these issues."

After parting from that meeting, John felt a rehabilitated sense of hope and optimism. As he walked back to his car, the uncertainty lifted slightly from his shoulders. He was fortunate to have run into Matthew, a stranger who possessed knowledge about economic issues and was genuinely interested in helping him succeed.

CHAPTER 8

❦

A Stark Revelation

John sat down in the wooden chair, nervously adjusting his watch. It was his first "Wealth Building" session with Matthew. The Ocean Cafe was minimally decorated, with large windows offering a panoramic view of the ocean. It was a cozy spot located in Pacific Beach, San Diego. John was checking out their menu, which was famous for its true Brazilian recipe in Acai bowls despite being known primarily as a juice shop and coffee destination.

As John scanned the menu, his mind wandered, distracted by the rhythmic sound of waves crashing against the shore. The smell of fresh coffee mingled with the salty ocean breeze, creating a calming and invigorating atmosphere. Just as John decided to order the Ocean Original Acai Bowl, Matthew arrived.

"Hey, John! Great to see you," Matthew greeted with a warm smile, extending his hand.

"Hi, Matthew. Thanks for meeting me here," John replied, shaking his hand firmly but nervously.

"No problem at all. I love this place. Have you been here before?" Matthew asked, settling into the chair opposite John.

"Actually, no. It's my first time. The view is amazing," John said, glancing out the window.

Matthew nodded. "It sure is. I come here often. The acai bowls are a must-try. Have you decided what to order?"

"Yes, I think I'll go with the Ocean Original Acai Bowl with a...latte," John said, pointing to the menu. "It has granola, banana, strawberry, honey, and blueberry."

"Good choice. I'll have the Hawaiian Acai Bowl," Matthew said to the approaching waiter. "And let's add a latte for John and an Americano for me."

As the waiter took their orders and left, Matthew turned his attention back to John. "So, how are you feeling about today's session?"

"Well...Hopeful against the odds," John said, adjusting his watch again.

"John, I've gathered you have financial expectations like everyone else," Matthew began, leaning forward slightly. "And, like most people, you haven't attained these dreams. More troubling is that you've done all you know to do to succeed. Also, having come from Jamaica, you thought financial success would be somewhat automatic just by landing in this country."

John nodded slowly; his expression reflected slight frustration but hope, too. "That's right, Matthew. I thought things would naturally fall into place with some effort and persistence."

"But recent experiences have caused you to rethink your position on money, business, wealth, etc. Isn't that true?" Matthew continued, his eyes meeting John's.

"Yes, it has. It's been tough, and I've had to confront some hard truths," John admitted, his voice tinged with vulnerability.

Matthew gave a knowing nod. "Given your situation, I'm sure you have reasons why you're not making financial headway. You might be thinking that one or more of the following conditions might be the problem: Low income, too much debt, can't save money, or the cost of living is too high."

John sighed deeply. "All of the above, honestly. It feels like I'm stuck in a cycle I can't break."

"If that's the case, have you found the root cause behind the issue?" Matthew asked, his tone gentle but probing.

John shook his head. "I wish I did. I've tried cutting expenses and picking up extra work, but nothing seems to help."

"There is no need to panic if you're not financially where you want to be," Matthew assured him. "The critical thing is that you've taken steps to change the situation, and I'm here to help you succeed."

John's eyes lit up with hope. "I really need that help, Matthew. I'm ready to do whatever it takes."

"But I must warn you," Matthew cautioned as his tone grew serious. "I believe some of the information we will go through will be somewhat uncomfortable. The topic concerns money, the most private thing in our lives. The things you've been told about money by your parents, friends, and the media will get in the way. And your way of handling money will also present a challenge. You've been accustomed to doing things a certain way, and you may have to make changes to succeed."

John nodded, indicating that he understood and was willing to comply with any suggestion that Matthew made.

Matthew smiled warmly. "That's the spirit, John. If you're experiencing financial difficulty today, shouldn't you be questioning the value of your past financial education and advice?" Matthew asked, his eyes locking onto John's.

John hesitated, then nodded slowly. "I suppose you're right. I've been following advice from all sorts of sources, but I'm getting nowhere."

Matthew continued, "As you will soon see, most people have a hard time saving money, struggling to make ends meet, and falling behind on debt payments."

John sighed, rubbing his temples. "That sounds exactly like my life right now."

"If you're experiencing these issues, it's time to open your mind to a different way of handling money. And because of our meetings, I believe you're ready to make changes," Matthew said, offering a reassuring smile.

"I am," John replied, "I'm ready to learn."

"Before diving into specifics, Matthew began, leaning back in his chair, "let's discuss our financial situation broadly. Currently, millions of us are optimistic about a bright financial future, but few are doing what is necessary to make these dreams come true. Instead, we haphazardly make financial decisions daily without considering their long-term consequences. We hope our financial situation will improve naturally as we move forward, but in the end, we're often surprised that it doesn't. This is because financial success isn't based on random financial habits. Good money management is a logical and common-sense system with much patience."

John, taking in every word, replied, "That makes sense. I've definitely been guilty of not thinking long-term."

"Yes, debt," Matthew said, picking up a report. "The Federal Reserve Board has observed that most Americans are cash-poor. Nearly half of us can't raise a small amount of cash for an emergency. This trend has remained consistent over the years with only minor changes."

John's eyes widened. "That's shocking. I had no idea it was that bad."

"That survey doesn't even include the poorest people," Matthew continued. "A significant portion of the population lives in poverty, struggling to make ends meet daily. When you combine the middle class and the poor, more than half of Americans are living on the financial edge."

John shook his head. "I never realized how widespread these issues were. It makes me feel less alone in my struggles."

Matthew nodded. "Exactly. You're not alone. The system makes it challenging for many to get ahead. Understanding these facts is the first step toward real change. For instance, nearly two-thirds of millennials live paycheck-to-paycheck. So, despite what we say and do, the clear message is that most of us are broke and don't know what to do about the situation."

John shook his head, eyes wide with disbelief. "Looks like no one around my age has any real financial stability."

Matthew agreed. "Exactly. And It's not just millennials. Household debt is at an all-time high, with significant amounts tied up in mortgages, student loans, auto loans, and credit card balances."

"It's hard to wrap my head around such facts," John said, visibly concerned.

…."The previous peak in national debt was during the Great Recession," Matthew continued. "This pattern proves that our debt continues to rise each year. We've come to rely on credit to pay for what we want after the bills consume all our available cash. In the long run, we spend more on the things we purchase because of the cost of credit."

John sighed deeply. "It's like a never-ending cycle. You need money, so you borrow it, thinking you can repay it after the next paycheck, but then you end up even deeper in debt."

"Yes, but the question remains: why do we fall into debt?" Matthew asked rhetorically, counting off reasons on his fingers. "Lack of cash, survival needs, emergencies, the desire to appear successful, keeping up with others, and poor financial planning. We constantly need money for what we want, and when we don't have the funds, we borrow it."

"And with borrowing comes bigger problems," John interjected, starting to see the pattern.

"Exactly," Matthew confirmed. "Excessive debt leads to a host of issues: inability to save, high-interest payments on borrowed funds, financial inflexibility, stress and anxiety, and ultimately, bankruptcy."

Matthew paused, letting his words sink in before continuing. "Speaking of it, bankruptcy is a significant issue. Each year, a vast – very vast number of people file for non-business bankruptcy. I believe it is over a million. The numbers fluctuate, but they remain consistently high."

John's brow furrowed. "That's a lot of people. I never thought I'd be the one to do it twice."

"The law prohibits a person from filing more than one bankruptcy petition in 10 years. For this reason, we must assume that the annual numbers represent a new batch of people each year," Matthew explained. "Most of these individuals probably never imagined they'd end up in bankruptcy court. But when we rely on credit as heavily as we do, it's almost inevitable."

John nodded slowly, the enormity of the situation dawning on him. "It's scary to think about. But I guess understanding this is the first step to avoiding it, right?"

"Absolutely," Matthew replied with a reassuring smile. "The goal is to make you aware of these realities so you can make informed decisions. Awareness is a tool. Knowledge is power, John, and now you have it. The next step is using it to break free from these cycles."

John leaned forward, his eyes focused intently on Matthew, who was about to go deeper into the grim realities of financial mismanagement.

"Our savings," Matthew began, his tone somber, "as you can imagine, our financial issues involve more than just debt complications."

John nodded, bracing himself for more unsettling facts.

"One major reason we get into debt is because we have no savings. Many of us are nervous about our financial future due to this lack of savings," Matthew continued, flipping through his little diary. "A significant portion of Americans are extremely or somewhat concerned about affording a comfortable retirement. Many have no retirement savings at all. A sizable number of Baby Boomers have very little saved for retirement, and nearly half of American adults have taken no steps to prepare for outliving their savings."

John's eyes widened in disbelief. "But how can so many people be so unprepared?"

Matthew nodded. "Years ago, our savings rate was more accommodating. Decades ago, we saved a substantial percentage of our income. Over the years, that rate has dropped significantly. Today, it's only a fraction of what it once used to be. We've never been great savers, and the data proves it."

John leaned back, absorbing the information. "Looks like we're moving in the wrong direction."

"Yes, most people are. While some progress has been made, few Americans have substantial savings," Matthew said. "Those who do tend to be in the upper echelon of the population."

"As you pointed out earlier, America is one of the wealthiest countries in the world. Yet so many of its people are struggling with money issues... Why?" John interjected.

"Exactly," Matthew agreed. "Despite all the money we make over our working lives, we end up broke and in debt by retirement. Most retirees depend heavily on Social Security for their income. The majority of us are living paycheck-to-paycheck, and many can't produce a small amount of cash for an emergency. Don't let the appearance of wealth deceive you," Matthew warned. "The great resumes, impressive college credentials, perfect careers, large incomes, big houses, and fancy cars are only illusions of wealth. Since most of what we have is purchased on credit, the lifestyle we portray is fake. More accurately, we make a lot of money but spend most on nonessential things and debt payments. So, essentially, we stay broke and retire poor."

John sighed. "It's like living in a house of cards. One wrong move and everything could come crashing down."

"Yes, a house of cards waiting to collapse. So, what does it mean to be broke?" Matthew asked rhetorically. "The definition is straightforward. You're broke when you're struggling to pay the minimum on your credit card balances, unable to cover the lien on your property, dreading the arrival of bills in the mailbox, unable to gather a small sum for emergencies, putting your next purchase on credit, and finding it hard to save anything from your paycheck. If any of these situations resonate with you, then you're broke."

John nodded slowly, a look of understanding dawning on his face. "That sounds all too familiar. Another way of saying the same is that most of us are working to die broke."

"That's exactly true, John," responded Matthew with certainty, "Being broke goes by many names: financial frugality, financial insecurity, financial distress, financial destitution," Matthew explained. "Call it what you will; the reality is that most of us are living on the financial edge year after year. Yet, this truth is often hidden, except from those who are dealing with it, which includes most of us. But we're incredibly quiet about the whole thing."

"Why?" John asked, genuinely curious.

"Because admitting to financial failure is humiliating, devastating for the ego, and downright shameful," Matthew replied. "Silence is our only protection. We mask the problem well. One way we do this is by shopping. As long as we can keep buying things on credit, we feel like we're financially solvent and making progress."

John shook his head. "It's a vicious cycle. Okay...I get the picture," he said after a moment of reflection. "What do I need to do to fix the problem?"

Matthew leaned forward, "The answer is both simple and complex. There isn't a single solution to becoming financially successful. It involves multiple steps. First, you need to understand what we're doing wrong. Next, you need to know how to fix these problems. Then, you need to apply corrective measures to start making progress."

"In other words, the solution goes deeper than just saying, 'I'm not making enough money,' 'I have too much debt,' or 'Things are too expensive,'" Matthew elaborated. "Our financial problem is more than what is seen on the surface. It's a cultural issue. We live in an economic environment designed to keep us broke. It's embedded in our educational system, our political system, our economic system, and our daily behavior. We struggle with many factors intended to keep us financially unstable."

John was intrigued. "Like what?"

"Many people are unaware of these factors; some ignore them, and others think they have the financial savvy to beat the odds. Meanwhile, millions of us work hard and make decent money but end up broke," Matthew explained. "The irony is that we all want financial success. This doesn't necessarily mean becoming rich, although it could. It means having enough money to travel without incurring debt, paying bills on time without stress, feeling secure about retirement savings, and handling emergencies without relying on credit cards."

"That sounds like a dream," John said wistfully.

"But achieving these goals has been difficult because most of us have been poorly educated about money, manipulated economically, socially, and politically, deceived about economic truths, and led to follow paths that benefit others more than ourselves," Matthew said firmly. "Knowing this, we need to be financially re-educated. This involves adopting a new perspective on money management and reevaluating our approach to debt, savings, investments, and banking systems. I hope you now have a clear picture of where most people are financially," Matthew concluded, his tone empathetic. "Your situation reflects a broader issue, but things can improve from here."

Just then, Matthew's phone buzzed on the table. He glanced at the screen and saw an important call coming in. "Excuse me for a moment, John," he said, picking up the phone.

"Yes, hello?" Matthew answered, his tone indicating the call's urgency. After a brief conversation, he hung up and turned back to John with an apologetic smile. "I'm sorry, John, but I have to take care of something urgent. We will continue this conversation soon—probably Friday. Is that okay with you?"

John nodded, a thoughtful expression on his face. "Yes, Friday works for me. Thank you, Matthew, for all the insights today. It's a lot to take in, but I appreciate your honesty and guidance."

Matthew stood up and extended his hand. "I'm glad we had this discussion, John."

John shook Matthew's hand firmly. "I'm looking forward to Friday. Thanks again, Matthew. Have a good day."

"You too, John. Take care," Matthew replied warmly.

As John walked out of the café, his mind buzzed with all the information he had just absorbed. The statistics, the harsh realities, and the steps toward financial recovery played over and over in his mind. He walked slowly to his car, replaying Matthew's words.

Sitting in his car, John took a deep breath. He looked out of the windshield, reflecting on his current financial situation. "It's a lot to process," he muttered to himself. "But I can do this. I have to."

Driving home, he thought about the changes he needed to make. The idea of creating a realistic budget, setting achievable goals, and tackling his debt seemed daunting but necessary. He remembered Matthew's reassurance that knowledge was power and felt hopeful.

CHAPTER 9

❦

Money And the Human Life Cycle

John came to their usual spot, the Ocean Café, a charming little place standing right by the coastline. The salty breeze and rhythmic crashing of the waves created a serene backdrop as he settled into his favorite corner table by the window.

John, already seated, glanced up from the menu as Matthew walked in. "Hey! Over here!" he called, waving him over.

Matthew smiled, weaving through the tables. "Hey, John. Already decided what to get?"

"Yeah, I just ordered my usual cappuccino. What about you?" John asked, gesturing for a waiter.

"I'll just get a black coffee," Matthew replied as the waiter approached, quickly placing his order. After exchanging a few pleasantries about their families and recent events, Matthew leaned forward, his expression growing serious.

"John, I was thinking that you may not realize it, but there's a lot that can be predicted about a person's financial future based on cultural trends or patterns," Matthew began, and John's brow furrowed in concentration.

Matthew continued before he could ask, "Well, unless you have a written plan to succeed financially, you'll do what most people do. More often, this means going through the daily grind and living the paycheck-to-paycheck lifestyle most people experience. And in the end, you'll have nothing to show for your hard work."

John nodded slowly, taking a sip of his cappuccino. "I hear you. But back to your point: how does culture affect your finances?"

"To see what I mean, let's assume that you were born and raised in the United States and not in Kingston, Jamaica. Allow me to fast forward your life, using various scenarios to make a point," Matthew suggested, leaning back slightly. "During the process, I'll show you the most likely path you would have taken from there and the outcome. This path is the broad road most people take to succeed."

John set his cup down, intrigued. "Alright, I'm listening."

Matthew took a deep breath and continued, "As we go through these illustrations, you'll gain some insight into your future in two ways: You'll see how easy it is to fall into a specific groove that will keep you living paycheck to paycheck. You will have seen what is likely to happen and can prevent it."

John's eyes widened, intrigued and a bit wary. "Okay, go on."

"In the United States and many other countries, adult life begins at 18. That was most likely true in your case. Before that, you were told what to do and when. So, from 0-18, you've been pushed, pulled, dictated to, and controlled by others...mostly your parents. When you turned 18, you felt liberated. You were free to step into the world as an adult and start living the life you wanted. Much of that included getting involved in late-night parties, free sex, illegal drugs, alcohol, and other things."

John raised an eyebrow, "Sounds familiar. So, what's the catch?"

Matthew leaned forward again with a slight smile, "As a free thinker, you had yet to learn where you came from and cared less about knowing. Seemingly, you suddenly appeared, and you were here to stay. More importantly, you felt invincible and in control of everything."

John chuckled softly. "Yeah, I remember feeling that way."

Matthew fixed his gaze on John, whose expression reflected curiosity and apprehension. The café's soft ambient music and the gentle ocean breeze contrasted sharply with the intensity of their conversation.

"You wanted to make a name for yourself," Matthew continued, "and you became passionate about a few

things, including the environment. You wanted to rid
the earth of all the pollution created by past generations.
That way, you could have a new beginning and get
things done your way."

John nodded, smiling, "It's hard to imagine with the
life I have lived, but yeah, I think I could be that kind of
person in a parallel universe."

Matthew smiled, too. "You felt so bright that the
world wasn't big enough to contain your wisdom. You
knew the answers to everything. Your parents seemed
out of touch with reality. Authorities were objects of
scorn. Your way of doing things was always the best."

John chuckled, "That's invincible."

"Exactly," Matthew agreed. "On the other hand, you
didn't take work seriously. Though the job provided
a paycheck, you had no desire to be loyal, prompt, or
dependable. On workdays, you did just enough to get
by and were prepared to walk away at the slightest
disapproval of your attitude and conduct. You were
free, had rights, and were ready to prove it."

John sighed, taking a sip of his coffee, "Hmm, wish
that was true."

"Well, you also believed in magic," Matthew went
on. "You held onto the belief that someday, wealth
would appear, and possessions would magically come
together. So, you felt no need to rush and get things
done. This was especially true about money. You had no
desire to save part of your earnings. 'Why save money,'

you often wondered, 'when you didn't have enough to spend?' You heard about investments, but you thought it was something that happens later in life. So, when you get older and more affluent, you will start the process."

John cleared his throat, "Well, that's a nice scenario."

Matthew nodded, "Then it happened. A sudden dose of reality jolted you. One day, you realized that being an adult wasn't as much fun as you had imagined. It requires courage to handle responsibilities and the backbone to accept the consequences of your actions. You also realize that nothing in life is free. This was especially true about success. People must work hard for what they want. And you would most likely have to do the same."

John leaned back, "Tough pill to swallow."

"About the same time, you had a new perspective about money," Matthew continued. "You realize that without it, life can be challenging. Besides, money gives people power, independence, and a higher quality of life. But to get it, there must be some legal tradeoff: selling a product, providing a service, or being employed by a company for wages. This meant you must get more serious about your future to accomplish anything."

John nodded, clearly engrossed in the conversation. "That's when I would have started thinking about my career more seriously."

"As part of your new revelation, you concluded that there are many paths to employment," Matthew said.

"Some people go to college and eventually end up on the job. Some join the military. Some enroll in trade schools. Others go directly into the workforce. Ultimately, the result is the same – a paycheck or money at the end of the month. And the more of it, the better."

John's interest was piqued. "But then what?"

Matthew took a deep breath. "Then, as you continued working and making money, you ran into another problem. You needed help holding onto some of the money you made. Seemingly, everything was spent on rent, food, car payments, auto insurance, gasoline, etc. Worse, the more you made, the more you spent. With so much to buy, there never seemed to be enough money to pay for everything. So, like most people, you decided to delay saving money because your needs demanded every dime you could find to buy what you wanted."

John frowned, recognizing the trap he had fallen into. "It's a vicious cycle."

"While these things were happening, you were aging but didn't realize it. You're now 25 years old," Matthew said, his tone somber. "Also, the idea of postponing your plan to save money created a new problem: You got closer to the poorhouse but didn't know it. A reality check: There are many ways to measure where an individual should be financially based on age."

John sighed, running a hand through his hair. "So what should the 25-year-old John do now?"

Matthew took a sip of his coffee, letting the rich aroma fill the air between them before continuing. "One of the best models I've seen is the Human Life Cycle and Financial Fitness Timeline," he said, leaning back in his chair. "With a small amount of money and a systematic approach to saving, the power of compounding interest can work wonders for a determined and patient individual."

John's mind was brimming with questions. He understood the concept of compounding interest but hadn't taken investment seriously until recently. Regretting not buying stocks when he had more disposable income, he was determined not to miss another opportunity. "And...what is the Human Cycle and Financial Fitness Timeline exactly?" he asked.

Matthew smiled. "It's a planning method that uses the system of compounding interest to measure where a person should be financially at different stages of life. The Human Life Cycle and Financial Fitness Timeline help a person be financially prepared for retirement by having reasonably enough liquid assets to sustain life comfortably. This, of course, assumes that the individual follows the plan."

John nodded thoughtfully. "What does the plan entail?"

"Well," Matthew began, "according to the timeline, between ages 18 and 24, your net worth should be about $25,000. Some people will have more, others less.

Most of this money should be cash, invested as liquid assets. Ideally, 80% should be marked for capital growth investment, and 20% should be invested in some income-producing fund."

John's eyes widened. "Twenty-five thousand? That seems impossible at that age."

"It does sound daunting," Matthew admitted, "but remember, this money is collected over time through regular savings and compounding interest. And, just in case you're thinking that you never had money to begin a savings program, may I remind you of something? American children between ages 4 and 12 receive a substantial amount of money annually... roughly $19 billion. While you may not have some of this money saved, we must assume that roughly a few of your age group do – those who learned the value of saving money early."

John sighed, thinking about the missed opportunities, "Oh. That's a missed boat. But all isn't lost, right?"

"Exactly," Matthew encouraged. "You still have time to make a big difference. Emerging from what seemed like a slumbering phase of your life, you realize you've missed some opportunities. But now, you're ready to make a change. You've promised yourself things will be much better moving forward."

John smiled, "So, at this point, I'm ready to settle down and get serious about this."

Matthew nodded approvingly. "Until now, your life has been simple. You're 25 years old and single. Though you've been living paycheck-to-paycheck, you have a job that provides a decent salary. You also have reliable transportation. Although your apartment is sparsely furnished, you're getting by. You're using a couch as a bed and have relied on fast food for sustenance."

"That is how it was once upon a time," John said, remembering his life when he was 25 years old.

"Soon, however, things change in ways you've never experienced," Matthew continued. "Though you like your freedom, you don't plan to live the rest of your life this way. You hope to get married someday and raise a family. But before you do, you want to be financially stable. At the same time, you realize that you can't wait until everything falls into place perfectly and then act."

"True," John agreed. "Life doesn't wait for perfect timing."

"Your thinking makes sense now, but only for a short time," Matthew warned. "Cultural influences and your emotions will get the best of you. Your parents' desire for grandchildren, your spouse's desire for children, and your own emotions will play tricks on your logic. Before long, you'll be married, have children, and postpone plans for financial readiness."

John frowned, remembering when he had her daughter, "I can see how that could happen."

"And as predicted, a year later, you got married," Matthew continued. "Your life has changed. You moved to a 2-bedroom apartment and bought furniture, entertainment systems, and kitchenware on credit. Now, you have higher rent, more credit card debt, student loans, car payments, and regular household expenses. Even with two incomes, things seem to have gotten complicated overnight."

John shook his head. "It's almost unbelievable how quickly things can spiral."

"Ten years later," Matthew went on, "you're now married with two children. You're settled in a career, living in a brand-new house, and depending heavily on credit cards to make ends meet. In one way, life appears to be going well. For outsiders, you have a great family, a lovely house, and a comfortable lifestyle."

John sighed deeply. "But financially, it's a mess, isn't it?"

"Yes," Matthew said softly. "Financially, you're feeling the pain of holding things together. Money is tight, and you don't know why. You've done everything right: two college degrees in the family, two great-paying jobs, two reasonably new vehicles. But you're struggling to stay afloat, and the stress of everything is taking its toll on your physical well-being."

John looked out the window at the crashing waves, lost in thought. "So, what should be done at that point? How can it be fixed?"

"Hold on, we'll get there," Matthew leaned back in his chair, his eyes scanning the serene ocean before settling on John's contemplative face. "Now, you're 35 years old," he continued, "According to the Human Life Cycle and Financial Fitness Timeline, between ages 34 and 35, your net worth should be roughly $50,000."

John's eyebrows knit together in concern. "Wish I was somewhere near that," he said wistfully.

Matthew nodded understandingly. "And that $50,000 excludes any equity in your home. Seventy-five percent of this money should be invested in a growth fund, and thirty percent should be allocated to an income and safety fund. But let's be real. During this time, your budget's two most expensive areas are housing and child-rearing. This is also when most people experience their highest debt levels due to these expenses."

John sighed, running a hand through his hair. "Yes, it's tough."

Matthew continued, "So, how are you doing in comparison? Do you have $50,000 saved for retirement? What about $25,000? Well... do you have at least $10,000 saved?"

John hesitated, then shook his head slowly. "Not even close. Maybe a thousand at best."

Matthew gave a reassuring smile. "If you have roughly $10,000 in savings, pat yourself on the back. Considering all the reasons to spend money, it's commendable to have stuck to a plan and saved at least this much. But if you haven't saved anything and your debt has increased, you might find your net worth hovering around zero, even with a 401(k)."

John's shoulders slumped. "It feels like going in circles."

"The need for more money is a common struggle," Matthew acknowledged. "Considering your current financial predicament, you've been quietly looking for another job. You spruced up your resume and landed a new job that pays significantly more than you currently make."

John's face brightened. "Yeah, I would feel like I could finally breathe."

Matthew smiled. "But that's not all. Your spouse also received a substantial pay increase due to a promotion. You both could hardly control your excitement. This was indeed a time for celebration, so you celebrated the event over dinner and wine."

John chuckled. "So, it would feel like everything was finally falling into place."

"As you inserted the numbers into the family's budget," Matthew continued, "you noticed a substantial increase over the previous months. Based on the figures, you intended to save money and eliminate some debt. But you also had a long list of things you wanted to buy. So, you manipulated the budget to make these things happen."

John nodded, his smile fading slightly. "Yes, thinking this was our chance to get everything we wanted."

Matthew's expression turned serious. "Looking at the budget more closely, you noticed room for a bigger house in a better neighborhood. You thought the family would thrive there. After discussing the issue with your spouse, you placed your house for sale. A month later, the house was sold, and you found the perfect replacement. You loved it – the vaulted ceiling, spacious backyard, private office, and other amenities gave you the feeling of success. 'Finally,' you would say to yourself, 'I'm moving up in the world.'"

John's face fell. "I remember that feeling, but it comes with a lot of new expenses."

"Right, with the increased income," Matthew went on, "you also felt the need to upgrade the cars. You did so for both vehicles. A more extensive television set was one of the items on your list, and you bought it. With these upgrades, you felt accomplished. You were living the American dream. But," Matthew added with a sigh, "there is a downside. Everything you own – the house, the cars, the television set, and the other toys – was purchased on credit. And although you haven't realized it, you've complicated your financial situation. From now on, you and your spouse will work long hours to pay for the upgrades. Occasionally, the thought of losing an income crosses your mind and your stress level spikes. Nevertheless, you take comfort in enjoying life while you can because you deserve it."

John looked away with a hint of regret in his eyes. "It seemed like a good idea at the time."

"With the new jobs," Matthew continued, "you and your spouse are busier. Your children are growing and demanding more from you each day. They want more of your time for extracurricular activities and more money for clothing, food, electronic devices, travel tickets, etc. At the same time, more money problems begin to surface. The extra debt you created is adding financial strain to the budget."

John nodded slowly. "I've felt that strain. It's overwhelming."

"Having more money by this time would be nice," Matthew said softly, "but this will be around for a while. You are broke again. Once again, you have a cash flow problem and don't know how it happened. You need more money to maintain your lifestyle, but getting it is a bigger problem. You considered getting a part-time job but can't handle the added stress and fatigue."

John sighed heavily. "And now the kids are graduating from high school, thinking about college."

"Exactly," Matthew replied. "Your kids are making college plans, but financially, you can't help them. It's a tough spot to be in, John. Now, it's several years later, and you, too, have aged. You're now 45 years old. According to the Human Life Cycle and Financial Fitness Timeline, your financial net worth should be about $150,000 in cash, excluding any home equity."

John nodded thoughtfully, absorbing Matthew's words. "That sounds like a lot of money. Sadly, I don't have anything close to that."

Matthew continued, "Half of this money should be dedicated to a growth fund, while 35% should be allocated to a safety and income fund. At this stage, you should also be re-evaluating other financial instruments like insurance policies, children's educational funds, and estate planning."

John furrowed his brow. "I haven't really thought about any of that. I've been so caught up with day-to-day expenses and keeping up with everything."

Matthew nodded sympathetically. "Given your situation, you're not alone in this—many people are in the same boat. In fact, most have around $5,000 or less."

John sighed, "I always thought I had time to figure it out later."

Matthew continued, "Unfortunately, unless something changes drastically—like a windfall of money—it's doubtful you'll meet the financial estimates set by the model. By age 54, for instance, your net worth should be about $300,000 in liquid assets, excluding home equity."

John nodded slowly as Matthew's words sunk in. "It's hard to think about all this. Life just seems to fly by."

"It does," Matthew agreed. "Ten years have passed since you bought your last house. Your children have graduated from college, likely with student loans, and now you have grandchildren. Yet, financially, things remain fragile. Your only hope is that you're still employed."

John grimaced, the reality hitting home. "Yes, it feels like I'm always trying to catch up."

Matthew nodded knowingly. "And even though you may have a $50,000 defined-contribution plan through your employer, your net worth still comes to zero when you factor in your high debt balance. Retirement age is fast approaching, and it seems less glittery than you had hoped."

John sighed deeply. "And I wouldn't feel ready to retire. Debt would keep me working for a long time."

"And now," Matthew continued, "you're 65 years old. At this juncture, your net worth should be about $400,000 and still growing. The focus shifts to capital preservation, with a significant portion allocated to an income and safety fund. It should also include long-term health care, disability insurance, liability insurance, social security income to supplement investment draws and estate planning."

John rubbed his temple with his thumb, "I can't even imagine having that much saved up."

Matthew's tone softened. "It's a common sentiment. Many people find themselves in similar circumstances as they near retirement. Social Security becomes a primary source of survival for many. In five years, you'll be 70 years old, and your financial condition is less likely to improve."

John frowned deeply. "Yes, I never thought it would come to this. I made good money over the years, but somehow, saving never seemed to happen."

Matthew nodded sympathetically. "It's a question many face. Where did the money go? What happened along the way? Now you find yourself broke, in debt, and uncertain how it happened."

John sighed heavily, "I wish I had taken financial planning more seriously."

John grimaced, the reality of his financial situation sinking in deeper. "It's a tough pill to swallow," he muttered. "I never imagined I'd be in this position."

Matthew offered a reassuring nod. "Fortunately, the scenario we've discussed hasn't happened to you yet," he said, his tone carrying a note of encouragement. "Although it's a harsh reality for millions, you're still in your 40s and have a chance to make a difference. You can prevent this problem from becoming your reality."

John nodded slowly, the gravity of Matthew's words not lost on him. "I get it now," he said quietly. "I need to change my approach. I can't afford to take things for granted anymore."

Sipping the last of his coffee, Matthew glanced at his watch and sighed regretfully. "I hate to cut this short, but

I've got to head out," he apologized. "Today's session was important. I hope you learned a lot."

John nodded. "Yes, I did," he replied earnestly. "Thank you for opening my eyes to all of this."

Matthew smiled warmly, "We'll continue our conversation next Friday. But before leaving, I want to say a few things..."

PRELUDE

※

(To Chapters 10-16)

" John, I know that you, like most people, want to know the 'one thing' that will make you financially successful—the secret to success, so to speak—and you want to get out there and put it into action and 'get rich quickly.' But the truth is, financial wealth doesn't come by knowing or doing 'one thing.' Rather, it comes through the discovery and application of many things."

John nodded, his curiosity piqued. "What do you mean by that?"

Matthew smiled gently. "In other words, you need to know what's preventing you from attaining and maintaining wealth and then make necessary improvements. And although some people get rich quickly, most people won't unless they change their habits and thinking about money."

John shifted in his seat, absorbing Matthew's words. "So, it's not just about finding a quick fix?"

"Nope," Matthew continued. "The real answer to your financial dilemma may not come from a book, magazine, or other written material but from several things; some of them are embedded in our culture, and others are inside you."

John furrowed his brow, trying to grasp the concept. "Can you give me an example?"

Matthew leaned back, considering his next words carefully. "In our next few sessions, we will unravel some of the cultural hindrances to financial progress that keep most people broke. Many of them are habits and customs intended to improve our lives, yet in many ways, they do more harm than good. They are deceptively designed to keep most people financially trapped for life."

John's eyes widened. "You mean, like societal expectations?"

"Yes," Matthew nodded. "Take, for example, the pressure to buy a home as a status symbol. While owning property can be a good investment, many people rush into it without considering the long-term financial commitment and potential pitfalls."

"That makes sense," John said thoughtfully. "I've seen friends struggle with mortgage payments, feeling trapped."

"Exactly," Matthew affirmed. "John, despite not being born in this country, your financial behavior has been influenced by its financial routes, impacting you, your children, other parents, and their children as well. If this cycle isn't broken, the financial outcome of their lives will predictably be the same."

John sighed, "So, how do we break the cycle?"

Matthew smiled warmly. "That's what we'll work on together. We'll identify those habits and customs that are holding you back and develop new strategies and mindsets that will set you on the path to financial freedom."

John felt a surge of determination. "I'm ready, Matthew. Let's do this."

They bid farewell, and John looked forward to the next session, feeling optimistic about his future despite his previous failures and setbacks.

CHAPTER 10

❧

Where Things Start Going Wrong

Matthew texted John that he wouldn't be able to make it to their meeting on Friday. "Some urgent work," he explained. John, understanding the importance of their discussion, suggested, "I can come to La Jolla if that's fine with you?" Matthew agreed, and they decided to meet the next day, which was Saturday.

The next morning, around 10 a.m., they found themselves at Caroline's Seaside Cafe, the same quaint spot where they first met. It was a charming place with outdoor seating near the coast, where the ocean waves crashed rhythmically against the shore, and seagulls filled the air with their beautiful calls. The sun was still at the horizon, casting a golden hue over the water and adding a warm glow to the morning.

John and Matthew found a quiet corner table that overlooked the beach, perfect for their third Wealth Building Session. The table was tucked away from the main flow of patrons, offering a sense of privacy and tranquility. The gentle sea breeze carried the scent of saltwater and freshly brewed coffee, mingling with the aroma of baked goods from the café.

As they settled in, the familiar comfort of the café provided a perfect backdrop for their conversation. John took a deep breath, feeling more at ease than he had during their first meeting. The sounds of the ocean and the distant chatter of other customers created a soothing ambiance. After scanning the menu, they placed their orders. John opted for a cappuccino and a breakfast croissant. Matthew chose a black coffee and a brioche French toast.

As they waited for their food, Matthew began, "John, I'm glad we're continuing these sessions. How have you been feeling about the steps we've taken so far?"

John smiled, feeling a sense of progress. "Honestly, I'm starting to see things differently. I've been more mindful of my spending habits and have started saving more consistently."

"That's great to hear," Matthew replied, nodding approvingly.

John thought for a moment before answering. "Well, it's been tough breaking some old habits. I didn't realize how ingrained they were. But I'm committed to making the changes."

Their conversation was briefly interrupted as the waiter brought their drinks and food. John's cappuccino was perfectly crafted, with a delicate layer of foam, and his breakfast croissant was golden and flaky. Matthew's black coffee emitted a robust aroma, and his brioche

French toast was beautifully presented with a dusting of powdered sugar and a drizzle of syrup.

"Looks delicious," John said, eyeing his croissant.

Matthew nodded, smiled, and took a sip of his coffee before he began, "John, our financial problems start when we're young. Most children in the United States and other countries grow up without financial education."

John nodded, listening intently.

"This is because neither parents nor schools teach kids about money," Matthew continued. "It's a cycle that's been going on for generations. When you look back over your own life, you may not have had good financial training growing up."

John reflected on Matthew's words and said. "You're right. I remember learning the value of hard work but not much about managing the money I earned."

Matthew sipped his coffee and added, "Exactly. Without a solid foundation in financial literacy, many people struggle to make informed decisions about their finances."

John took a sip of his cappuccino, savoring the frothy richness before responding, "So, what do you think needs to change? How do we break this cycle?"

Matthew looked out the window, contemplating the waves crashing against the shore. "Financial illiteracy in our youth is the first cultural barrier to financial success. You didn't know it then, but this oversight has significantly impacted your ability to handle money well."

John nodded slowly, "I never learned how to manage it properly when I was young."

"Exactly," Matthew replied. "For instance, if you're having financial difficulty today, it is mainly due to a lack of sound financial training in your childhood. Child psychologists tell us that kids learn most of what they need to know between 0 and 12."

"That makes sense," John said, thinking back to his own childhood.

"During these years, kids mimic both good and bad behaviors from their parents and friends. These behaviors become rudimentary habits for life," Matthew explained.

John sipped his cappuccino, lost in thought.

Matthew continued. "Kids are impressed mainly through visual imagery rather than spoken language. Even as adults, we react the same way. 'Don't tell me,' we say, 'show me.' So, as human beings, we tend to repeat what we see... not necessarily what we hear."

John nodded again, a look of realization dawning on his face. "So, left on my own, I formed my perception about money based on what I saw and experienced."

"That's right, John," Matthew continued. "As a child, you regularly visited the store and supermarket with your parents and enjoyed them. You were mesmerized by the variety of products on the shelves. You wanted all of them: toys, candy, food, and more. Occasionally, your parents would buy you an item, making your day. From there, you associate money with the things you want."

John chuckled softly, remembering those trips to the store. "I do recall those times. I guess that's where it all started."

"Studies show that kids between 4 and 5 begin expressing their wishes," Matthew went on. "During that time, roughly two-thirds of children ask for things they see on television. At the same time, they start memorizing the locations of certain products in the store. Before age 5, they also learn specific survival techniques, one of which is the art of manipulation."

John raised an eyebrow. "Manipulation?"

"Yes," Matthew nodded. "They discover that a particular behavior will produce positive results. Parents would capitulate under pressure and give them what they want. So, that behavior became a game. When they don't get what they want, they throw tantrums. I'm sure you've seen this conduct many times, and you most likely did the same thing at that age."

John laughed. "Oh, definitely. I've seen it with my kids and remember doing it myself."

"At age 5, kids become self-directed shoppers. They know what they want and influence their parents to buy it. As a result, advertisers are bypassing parents and pitching certain products directly to kids. Corporations spend billions of dollars annually advertising certain goods to children ages five and older. The results are predictably positive for these companies."

"That's a staggering amount," John remarked. "And it works because kids are such a strong influence on their parents' buying decisions."

"Exactly," Matthew agreed. "By age 6, children begin to understand the value of money. The various denominations begin to make sense, and they learn to associate money with the things they want. By eight years old, kids' perception of things for pleasure and fun gets much larger. Their choice of candy expands; their toy selection becomes more expensive, and spending increases exponentially."

John shook his head, amazed. "It's incredible how early these patterns start."

"During the same time, children begin to be influenced by brand-name products," Matthew added. "They become impulsively connected to specific clothing, logos, and designs. At that age, their appetite for money also intensifies. They want more of it to spend. So, they begin to deal with their parents for allowances and other ways to earn money. Often, this includes doing small jobs around the house for pay."

John sighed, leaning back in his chair. "It all makes so much sense now. I can see how those early experiences shape our future financial habits."

Matthew took a bite from his muffin and continued, "John, the amount of money kids between ages 4 and 12 earn annually amounts to billions, which is staggering. It comes from various sources: allowances, working around the house, gifts from parents and relatives, and doing neighborhood chores."

John nodded, intrigued. "And where does all that money go?"

"Unfortunately, most of it gets spent on things like clothing, snacks, movie tickets, entertainment systems, and electronic devices," Matthew explained. "Very little, if any, is put into savings."

John sighed, shaking his head. "It's hard to believe, but I guess it's not surprising."

"Think of it this way," Matthew continued. "It wasn't long ago when you were 12 years old. You, too, had access to some amount of money at that time. How much of it do you have today?"

John chuckled ruefully. "None of it."

"As you have discovered," Matthew said, "money won't stay with people who aren't trained to handle it properly. Having access to a great deal of money at any age doesn't equate to success. When managed poorly, money flies away. It simply disappears."

John nodded in agreement. "That's a hard lesson I've had to learn."

"Here is another fundamental truth," Matthew continued. "Your expense is someone else's income. This means that the more you spend, the more you increase the wealth of others. As far back as you can remember, making money hasn't been easy. But even then, you had more difficulty saving it."

"That's true," John admitted. "I tried to save once or twice, knowing it was the right thing to do. But my desire to spend was much stronger."

"Exactly," Matthew said. "Eventually, you succumbed to the idea that you couldn't save money. You thought only grown-ups could do it. So, you decided to wait until you became an adult to start saving. Meanwhile, you kept spending, buying the things you wanted when the mood was right."

John smiled sheepishly. "That sounds about right. The habit comes naturally."

"It was much easier doing what your parents, friends, and others did with their income – buying things," Matthew said. "No one saved any money. If they did, they didn't talk about it. So, you did the same thing. You didn't know it then, but as you look back, just as you got hooked on phonics, you should have been trained in money management. That aspect of your training was ignored or didn't seem important at the time."

"Yeah, I guess I do tend to blame my parents for my financial troubles," John admitted.

"But the issue goes much deeper than that," Matthew pointed out. "Financial illiteracy in children is a cultural issue. It goes back through generations. The topic of money has always been, and still is, highly secretive. People don't like to discuss the subject because it reveals their vulnerability: embarrassment, impulsiveness, indebtedness, low savings."

John leaned forward, listening intently. "So, we stay quiet about it, which just perpetuates the problem."

"Yes, sadly," Matthew said. "Who else should be blamed for your financial issues? The correct answer is our culture. In this case, everyone is responsible: parents, schools, the government, the media, companies, friends, and even you. That's right. All of us are at fault."

John sighed deeply. "Even today, most children leave home without a good financial education."

"Did you and your wife take the time to show your children how to manage money well?" Matthew asked pointedly.

John shook his head. "No, we didn't. It seemed too complicated, and we were embarrassed about our own struggles."

"That's a common problem," Matthew said, counting the reasons on his fingers. "Financial experts agree that most parents avoid the topic for several reasons: it's too complicated, they are ashamed to admit their weaknesses with money, or they lack the discipline to manage their financial affairs. When the issue is addressed, it's often in reaction to a problem like excessive spending or debt."

John looked thoughtful. "So, kids grow up financially illiterate because no one teaches them."

"Exactly," Matthew said. "The assumption among many parents is that as children age, they naturally become money-smart. But that's not the case. People don't necessarily become financially intelligent because they are older. The process requires training, practice, self-control, and discipline. Children who miss these rudimentary concepts become teenagers void of financial sense."

John nodded. "That explains a lot. Most teenagers I know don't seem to have a clue about managing money."

"Year after year, surveys show that most teenagers don't know how to manage money," Matthew continued. "They have no problem making and spending it, but they lack sound financial judgment. Most of what they buy has little intrinsic value – fashion apparel, cars and accessories, electronic games, movie and concert tickets, smartphones, school dances, spring break trips, fast food, and expensive dates."

John sighed again. "From a marketing standpoint, this is excellent news. Companies know what teenagers want and what inspires them to spend. But it's disastrous for the kids."

"Yes, exactly," Matthew agreed. "For most teenagers, money has one purpose – something to use in exchange for what they want. This attitude is not only misleading but also long-lasting. It's carried over into adulthood and is often the source of many financial complications later in life."

John looked up with a spark of hope, "So, Is there a way to turn this around?"

"There is good news," Matthew said with a smile. "You can still make substantial financial progress despite what has happened to you economically. By sitting here with me, you've demonstrated that you're serious about your financial future. At this point, you should determine – once and for all – to end your financial setbacks. This means looking ahead for a brighter future. But I must warn you, curbing your desire to spend will not be easy. You will struggle to beat back today's marketing schemes to keep you spending. Your desires will be your worst enemy."

John straightened up, "Daily, I'll battle with urges to spend. But I must subdue these impulses if I want to improve my financial condition."

Matthew nodded, his expression supportive. "If you consistently apply some of the things you learn during our meetings, you'll become financially independent."

"This sounds good," John replied with a smile. "I'm so eager to change my economic condition and take control of my financial future."

"John, as I recall, you have two children (boy and girl) graduating from high school soon and getting ready for college," Matthew asked thoughtfully after a brief pause. "Is that correct?"

John nodded, "Yes."

"Great!" Matthew responded, "Then, you still have time to make a difference in their lives today and in the future through financial literacy."

"What I'm about to say," continued Matthew, "is also applicable for parents with smaller children."

John nodded, "I know what you mean, Matthew. I've been thinking about this a lot, especially with college expenses hovering above."

Matthew leaned forward. "I always feel that parents should do more to prepare their children for economic success by taking a broad view of the problem and thinking about how they can fix it. Today, most of our population faces economic insecurity, primarily due to financial illiteracy, with far-reaching consequences. You and your family may unknowingly contribute to this problem, but there are steps you can take now to make a significant positive impact."

John sipped the last of his cappuccino, his eyes narrowing in thought. "So, what can I do? It feels overwhelming."

Matthew continued, "By improving your financial condition and honestly conveying your progress to your children, you can help them improve theirs and benefit the community simultaneously. Most people are unaware of this, but decades of financial secrecy and the lack of financial education at home have led to widespread economic dysfunction. This problem has grown to epidemic proportions, affecting people's health, relationships, emotional well-being, and overall happiness."

John sighed. "I've been there. Financial stress can tear families apart."

"Exactly," Matthew agreed. "Financial struggles do not only impact individuals but also their families, friends, and communities. Financial stress can decrease social interactions, cause family arguments, lead to divorces, and burden the community through legal and government assistance."

John looked down at his empty coffee cup. "It's a heavy burden. But where do I start?"

"Addressing financial illiteracy starts with you taking proactive steps if you're facing economic difficulties," Matthew explained. "This involves seeking financial education—as you are now doing—acquiring relevant skills, and getting coached for economic improvement. This proactive approach is crucial, especially if your children depend on you for guidance."

"Being a financial role model sounds like a big responsibility," John said.

"It is," Matthew said, nodding. "But changing your financial behaviors can significantly benefit the ones closest to you. Here are some actions you can take:

- Decide to bring permanent, positive changes to your financial life.

- Admit to your children that you're struggling financially and are working to improve the situation.

- Pursue financial education, training, or coaching, and inform your children about your plans.

- Reduce impulse spending and explain your reasons to your children.

- Limit credit card use and demonstrate the benefit of waiting to buy something until you can afford it.

- Save a portion of your income and show your children how it's done.

- Pay your monthly bills on time and let your children see the process.

- Avoid buying unnecessary items, even if everyone else has them.

- Talk about long-term goals like living in a better neighborhood or investing.

- Take action to achieve them.

- And most important of all, remain committed to your financial plan despite minor setbacks.

Following these guidelines can help you work toward financial stability," Matthew concluded.

John took a deep breath. "It sounds like a lot of work, but I can see how it would make a difference."

Matthew smiled encouragingly. "Remember, without change, your financial situation will remain the same. But, taking these steps can lead to significant improvements within three to five years."

John sat up straighter. "And how do I train my kids to manage money?"

"Teaching kids about financial responsibilities early in life helps them develop sound judgment for making informed financial decisions as adults," Matthew explained, "Parents are ideally suited for this task. Those with young children should begin financial training as early as age five by teaching them to manage money earned through chores and other means."

"But my children are older than five," John replied somberly, wondering if he was too late.

"I understand, John," Matthew reassured him. "This is a general guideline for parents. Regardless of their age, you can teach your children critical financial principles such as…

- Save a portion of their money for future investments.
- Donate to charitable causes of their choice.
- Contribute a small amount to household expenses to learn responsibility.
- Spend wisely on desired items.

Furthermore, parents should explain the benefits of each action to their children to ensure they understand the importance of these habits."

"And what about when they get older, as in my situation, for example?" John asked.

"When your teenager starts earning money outside the home, encourage them to continue the financial habits they learned as children, assuming they are familiar with the basic steps I just mentioned; if not, start here," Matthew said. "They should continue saving for wealth building and large purchases, cover their needs, and handle their own bills while they're living with you. These things can be done with or without supervision, preparing them to handle financial realities safely at home."

John looked thoughtful. "It sounds like a good plan. It will take some effort, but it's worth it."

Matthew nodded. "Absolutely. However, it may seem harsh if your children are not used to this kind of training. Avoiding it perpetuates financial illiteracy and eventual failure. Helping your children develop the necessary financial skills for success should be a top priority. This training will enable them to make informed financial decisions, handle immediate responsibilities, spend wisely, invest for growth, and save for retirement."

John smiled. "Thanks, Matthew. This gives me a lot to think about and work on. I'll start making these changes for me and my kids."

"You're welcome, John," Matthew said, patting his friend on the back. "Following these recommendations will benefit you, your children, and the community. You will contribute to financial wellness in your home, prepare your child for economic health, and help end the financial illiteracy epidemic in our country."

Matthew looked at his watch and said, "It's time I go now, John. It was an engaging session."

"It was. Thank you for the time, Matthew. See you next week." John smiled.

"See you, John."

CHAPTER 11

❦

College: A Path to Success or Failure?

Matthew called John on Thursday for the next wealth-building session.

"Hey, John. How's it going?" Matthew's voice sounded excited over the phone.

"Hey Matthew, I'm good. What's up?" John replied, curious about the call.

"I'm going sailing tomorrow, and I thought you might want to join me," Matthew said. "We'll be heading out from Shelter Island Drive."

"Sailing? That sounds amazing! Count me in," John said eagerly.

"Great! Be there by 10 a.m. You'll love it," Matthew said before they ended the call.

The following day, he arrived at the location. As he approached the marina, he saw a board that read, "Sailing San Diego." He looked ahead at the docked boats and yachts, taking in their sleek designs and polished surfaces glistening in the sunlight.

From one particularly luxurious yacht, John noticed Matthew waving at him enthusiastically. John walked toward the impressive vessel, its name proudly displayed on the side: "BAVARIA 46 SAILING YACHT." His eyes widened with amazement at the sheer size and elegance of the yacht.

"Wow, this is incredible!" John exclaimed as he stepped onto the deck.

"Welcome aboard, John!" Matthew greeted him warmly, shaking his hand. "Glad you could make it."

The yacht began slowly moving away from the docks, the engine purring smoothly as they ventured into the open waters. Once they reached the open waters, Matthew hoisted the sails and stopped the engine. The sails usually require some attending depending on the wind force and direction of travel, but fortunately, the wind was low and the sea calm, allowing the two men to sit and converse without too much distraction. John felt a rush of excitement and liberation as the city skyline receded into the distance. The gentle rocking of the yacht and the cool breeze against his face made the experience even more exhilarating.

"Can you believe this view?" John said, marveling at the vast expanse of blue water and the horizon stretching endlessly before them.

"It's something, isn't it?" Matthew replied, leaning casually against the railing. "It's the perfect setting for our discussion today."

As they sailed farther from the shore, Matthew began thoughtfully, "Imagine a culture where most parents are broke and struggling to maintain the lifestyle they've created on credit. They are exhausted by multitasking all day, highly stressed by financial demands, and doubtful about their financial future. Yet, their children, who have little or no financial skills, are ready for college and need help."

John nodded, listening intently as Matthew continued. "The cost of a four-year university is exceptionally high, and neither the parents nor the children have the money to pay for this highly anticipated undertaking. The only option is to borrow the money to pay for college. But more often than not, the ones who must shoulder the financial burden are the students, not the parents."

John's expression grew thoughtful. "It's a tough situation. I remember going through that myself."

"Exactly," Matthew said. "You, too, have gone to college on borrowed money. So, what would you do? On one hand, hopeful college students can dismiss the idea altogether and try to find work without a degree. But since they believe the college degree will help them succeed, they'll do what most people do – go to college."

John gazed out at the water, contemplating the dilemma. "It looks like a catch-22. You need the degree to get ahead, but the debt can hold you back for years."

Matthew nodded and gestured toward an array of coolers brimming with various drinks and a large box overflowing with snacks. He picked up a bag of Hawaiian Kettle Chips, the crinkling bag adding a satisfying sound, and a juice box. Meanwhile, John reached for some rice crisps and a can of ginger ale; the cool metal of the can felt refreshing against his hand.

"These look good," John said, popping open his Ginger Ale.

"Yeah, they're my favorite," Matthew replied, crunching on a chip. "Let's get back to our discussion."

As they snacked, Matthew continued from where he left off. "The pursuit of a college degree is the second cultural barrier to financial success. In affluent countries such as ours, most children have been prepared for college. This is so because the culture promotes success through a degree."

John nodded, taking a sip of his drink. "It's like we're all set on this one track from a young age."

"Yes," Matthew agreed. "The common thinking is that you will get ahead if you obtain a college degree, find a promising career, and work hard. But how well does this formula work for the masses?"

"Not as well as we'd hope," John said thoughtfully. "A lot of people I know are struggling despite having degrees."

Matthew sighed. "Apparently, millions of people have followed this plan, hoping to attain their financial dreams by the time they retire. Instead, what often happens is that most of them end up broke, in debt, and looking toward Social Security to survive during retirement."

"So what's wrong with this well-promoted blueprint for success? Is it flawed?" John asked, leaning in.

"That's the big question," Matthew said. "Is it possible that the type of education that students get from college is ill-suited for individual success? Are there other negative implications about higher education that most people ignore before committing to the program?"

"If this is true," John mused, "many more people will follow the same plan with great optimism, only to be disappointed."

"Exactly," Matthew said, nodding. "To answer these questions, look at the college degree for clarification. From the get-go, no one can deny the value of a good education. Knowledge in science, business, government, social studies, and others is fundamental to a balanced view of life. Education empowers people."

"It really does," John agreed. "But is it necessary to go to college to get a good education?"

"Of course not," Matthew said firmly. "Knowledge is a means to know or become aware of things. It's a process that gradually develops...line upon line, precepts upon precepts. It happens over time through training, observation, and experiences. This means that the entire process is a universal endowment that occurs over a lifetime. Therefore, no one place or institution holds the absolute right to higher education."

"So we can tell people that going to college or a university is optional for financial success?" John asked.

"Exactly," Matthew replied. "Many of our time's great leaders, planners, and thinkers had no more than a high school diploma. Some had no formal education or certification. They were self-educated visionaries who eventually changed our world. Here is a short list of people who fall into this category:" Matthew counted on his fingers as he continued, "Thomas Edison, Abraham Lincoln, The Wright Brothers, Charles Lindbergh, Walt Disney, Bill Gates, and Steve Jobs."

John's eyes widened. "That's quite a list. It's inspiring to think about."

"Even so," Matthew continued, "most people feel they need a college degree to succeed. This is so because the culture promotes the idea. But realistically, college is not meant for everyone. In fact, fewer people should chase the degree than those who do."

"That makes sense," John said, nodding. "But what about job requirements?"

"Yes, apart from the prestige of the college degree, its primary purpose is to fulfill job requirements," Matthew explained. "Employers, increasingly exposed to market competition, need to hire intelligent individuals to stay in business. Supposedly, college grads are more prepared to fill these positions than those with no degrees. Parents who want their kids to have a better life encourage them to pursue higher education for this purpose. For the same reason, many adults who don't have degrees make their way to college."

"So we cannot deny that colleges and universities provide qualified candidates for the job market," John concluded.

"Yes, but despite all the excitement that surrounds the college degree, is a person better off economically with it or without it?" Matthew asked rhetorically, "Most would quickly say, 'Yes, it makes financial sense to get the degree.' Yet, ironically, the economic results of most college graduates tell a different story.' It is not uncommon for college students to sit in sanitized classrooms and daydream about the world. Four years of thumbing through textbooks, doing case studies, and listening to professors is much time to think about political, social, and economic issues. Pre-graduate income expectation is the most unrealistic view among likely college graduates. Many undergraduate students expect their income to increase drastically after graduation."

John leaned back, contemplating Matthew's words. "It's a lot to think about. It really challenges the way we've been taught to see education and success."

"That's the point," Matthew said with a smile. "We need to question these ingrained beliefs and find what truly works for us individually. MBA graduates often have high expectations for their salaries post-graduation. Many look forward to earning significant sums such as

$100,000 in the first year, double that much in five years, and three times that amount in around ten years."

John raised an eyebrow. "Those are some big numbers."

Matthew nodded. "In truth, people who attend college generally stand a better chance of making more money than those who don't. But those top earnings are reserved for a select few."

"Like who?" John asked.

"Statistically, only a small percentage of college graduates can make more than $300,000 annually," Matthew explained. "Many of these individuals are lawyers, physicians, and high-level executives. Similarly, only a fraction of MBA graduates will reach this income level within five to ten years after graduation, depending largely on their experience and specific occupation. You could be one of these high-income earners, but it's far from guaranteed."

"That makes sense," John said, crunching on his Rice Crisps. "But what about the majority?"

"Most college graduates will earn much less than they anticipate," Matthew replied. "The average starting salary for college grads is around $45,000 a year, with modest annual increases. At this rate, it takes several years to reach a six-figure income."

John frowned. "But that's quite a gap from those high expectations."

"yes, it is," Matthew said. "According to Pew Research, most graduates still think college was worth it. This opinion spans the largest US generations — Boomers, Gen-Xers, and Millennials. They agree that college has either paid off or will pay off, given the investment."

"The highest-earning graduates were the most positive, right?" John asked.

"Yes," Matthew confirmed. "Those making six figures and up overwhelmingly felt their degree had paid off, compared to a smaller percentage of graduates earning less than $50,000 a year. So, when we measure the college degree solely on income potential, there's a clear financial benefit."

"Oh," John said. "But I remember you mentioned another factor to consider before enrolling."

"Indeed," Matthew said. "The method by which tuition is paid, which most often involves credit, is crucial. Although this issue is given less weight in favor of anticipated income, it often determines financial success or failure. Because most people are cash-poor, they rely on credit to fund their college education. This should be the number one concern about enrolling in college because, in the end, the debt created to obtain the degree can become a significant burden."

John looked concerned. "So, we need to look at the debt aspect more closely."

"Absolutely," Matthew said. "We'll discuss this in more detail later. For now, consider that a college degree provides no guarantee of a job or high salary. Many more college graduates make less than $50,000 a year than those who make six figures."

"That surely is an eye-opener," John admitted.

"And remember," Matthew continued, "a high income doesn't necessarily equate to financial success. For example, someone earning $200,000 a year may not be better off financially than someone earning $50,000, depending on how they manage their money."

"Well, that's true," John agreed. "Managing money is the real game."

"Exactly,' Matthew said. "All the same, I congratulate you and all those who have attained a college degree. It's an outstanding achievement, and I hope you're now reaping the benefits of your efforts, especially in terms of higher income. But basing the value of the degree solely on income without considering the debt incurred is a one-sided measurement….The cost should also be considered, and for most people, that includes the credit used to pay for the education."

John nodded thoughtfully. "That's a good point. Debt can really weigh you down."

"As I mentioned earlier," Matthew continued, "the student loan application process is easy and accommodating because credit is how most students can pay for higher education. Just about every applicant can qualify for a loan because the US government guarantees a large percentage of it. This means there's little or no risk for lenders who advance student loans."

"But going to college is expensive," John noted.

"Very true," Matthew agreed. "You have attended a university, and you know that to be true. Tuition varies from one institution to the next, and the price goes up each year. The average published tuition and fees for a four-year public education are approximately $10,000 annually. For out-of-state students, it increases significantly. The cost of attending a private college is even higher. Some reports show the figures are as high as $40,000 a year. It's a costly undertaking, which is why understanding the financial implications is so important."

John sighed, taking in all the information.

Matthew continued, "More often, it's the student who must bear the financial burden of going to college. Recent surveys show that a significant portion of undergraduates who attend both public and private colleges end up relying heavily on student loans."

John, munching on his Rice Crisps, nodded thoughtfully. "I know a few friends who are already stressing about their loans, and they haven't even graduated yet."

Matthew leaned back, taking a sip of his juice. "It's a common story. For those who desire to pursue a graduate program, the cost is even higher. Many advanced degree holders owe staggering amounts for their education. The system is designed in such a way that everyone involved benefits. Colleges stay busy issuing diplomas; students fill the classrooms despite the costs, employers get to hire educated candidates, and degree holders earn paychecks."

John interjected, "And there's the dark side of student loans."

"Absolutely," Matthew confirmed. "The student loan is a part that should concern you the most. The credit taken out for the degree becomes a debt, and the student is responsible for repaying it. For many degree holders, this debt is financially threatening. It lingers for years after graduation, hinders financial progress, and contributes to a significant portion of trillions of dollars in student loan debt in the United States."

John's eyes widened. "I had no idea it was that much."

Matthew nodded. "And student loan default is a serious issue. Many graduates have difficulty repaying their loans, and some experts believe this could be the next financial crisis."

"That sounds pretty scary," John said.

"It is," Matthew agreed. "For many students, obtaining a college degree has been a bittersweet experience. Imagine starting life with this kind of financial burden. It's like being stuck in a muddy pit, trying to climb out but slipping back down."

John frowned, "And it doesn't end with just student loans, does it?"

"No, it doesn't," Matthew replied. 'This is often just the beginning of a lifetime of debt. Cars, houses, furniture, and more are typically purchased on credit, adding to the already painful college ordeal. So, while many college grads are happy to have their degrees, they are drowning in debt and struggling to see a way out. They feel they'll never buy a house, raise a family, or achieve financial freedom, partly because of their student loans and credit card debt."

John sighed, "Looks like a trap."

"It can feel that way," Matthew acknowledged. "And the laws make it difficult to discharge student loans through bankruptcy. While there are some cases where loans can be forgiven, the debt usually stays with the individual until it's fully paid off or they pass away. Payments are due shortly after graduation, but many students are not financially prepared to handle the repayments."

"What happens then?" John asked.

"This situation often leads to loan delinquencies or forbearances, which add more interest to the balance," Matthew explained. "And student loans are just one part of the debt burden. On campus, financial demands are endless. High-priced textbooks, transportation, food, and other fees keep students spending on credit. With little or no income, most students rely on credit cards, racking up even more debt."

John shook his head, "It's a lot to manage."

Matthew looked at John and asked, "So, what would you say? Is the college degree a financial way up or down? While it may initially appear as a way up, when obtained through credit, it becomes a financial ambush. Often, it's the first heavy debt obligation young people incur, which complicates their ability to start and grow their lives. When two people start a family, both might be saddled with student loans, making it difficult to get ahead."

"Well, that's discouraging," John said quietly.

"The college degree itself isn't the problem," Matthew clarified. "It's the method used to obtain it that creates the burden. This financial strain gets in the way of progress and lingers for years after graduation. And the sad part is few people care about the financial challenges of college graduates. Not the government, companies, schools, the media, friends, or even family members. Employed or unemployed, the individual must bear this burden alone."

John sighed, "No wonder most college graduates are living paycheck-to-paycheck."

"Exactly," Matthew said. "Despite the promise of a high salary after graduation, most are just as broke as everyone else. The system needs a serious reevaluation if we're to find a sustainable way forward for future generations."

Suddenly, John's eyes widened as he spotted movement in the water. "Look, Matthew! Dolphins!" he exclaimed, pointing towards the bow.

A pod of dolphins had appeared. Their grey bodies glided effortlessly through the water. The dolphins swam alongside the yacht, their fins slicing through the surface. They leaped and dove, performing an aquatic ballet that left John awestruck. Their playful clicks and whistles echoed through the air, sounding almost like laughter.

"Wow," John breathed, leaning over the railing to get a closer look. The dolphins circled the yacht, almost as if they were curious about the visitors, before continuing on their way, disappearing into the deep blue.

Matthew watched John's amazement with a smile. "Nature's little surprises," he said. "Always a reminder of the beauty and wonder around us."

John nodded, still captivated by the encounter. "I've never seen dolphins up close like that."

Matthew gestured toward the box of snacks and coolers. "Grab something to eat. Let's get back to our discussion." They picked up fruit bars each

As they settled back into their seats, Matthew continued, "Here's what I would recommend. People who don't have a college degree and feel uncomfortable about their level of education should do something about it. But this doesn't mean going to college. Not everyone should obtain a degree. As I said at the beginning of this discussion, fewer people should go to college than those who do."

John chewed on his fruit bar, which had an apple and twelve strawberries, while listening intently.

"If they feel they must attend a university," Matthew said, "they should remember that things may not work out as expected after graduation. Most college graduates encounter four major problems after graduation: debt accumulation, lower-than-expected income, few graduates working in their major, and the aging of the degree."

John's brow furrowed. "So, what's the alternative?"

Matthew leaned back, taking a thoughtful sip from his juice box. "If someone needs to pursue a college degree, they should consider doing so while employed by a company that will pay part or all of the tuition. That way, they won't end up in debt after graduation. For example, people who enlist in the US military have direct access to tuition assistance. Other companies offer similar benefits."

John looked intrigued. "What about other options besides college?"

"It's crucial to move away from the notion that college is the only path to financial success," Matthew said. "Consider these alternatives: Military training provides excellent specialized training. Vocational education focuses on practical training for specialized jobs like engineering, architecture, carpentry, and medicine. Professional certificate programs offer a low-cost approach to higher education. And then there's self-directed learning, which is unconventional but highly effective."

John leaned forward, clearly interested. "So, the primary purpose of education is to improve your standard of living, right?"

"Yes, exactly," Matthew agreed. "The knowledge gained should enable you to become more marketable in the workforce, make better career choices, earn more income, and become more prudent with your finances. The most important thing is not to let the culture dictate your educational path. The choice is yours and yours alone. Choose a path that prevents any debt accumulation. Accumulating debt while going to college is a way down for most people, not up."

John sighed, nodding slowly. "It makes sense. There's so much pressure to follow the traditional route, but it's clear that it's not the only way."

Matthew smiled warmly. "It's all about making informed decisions that align with your goals and financial well-being."

The sun hovered right above their heads now, creating sparkles over the waves as the yacht began to turn back towards the shore. John took a deep breath, feeling more enlightened and optimistic about the future. The dolphins were long gone, but their brief appearance had added a magical touch to an already enlightening day.

Two hours had flown by, and as the yacht approached the dock, John felt a sense of fulfillment. "This has been a wonderful experience," he said, looking at Matthew.

"Thank you for the insights and the amazing time on the yacht."

Matthew smiled, patting John on the back. "Anytime, John. The journey to financial success is about making smart, informed choices. And sometimes, it's about enjoying the journey along the way."

CHAPTER 12

⚜

A Modern Enslaving Apparatus

On a bright Friday morning, John was eagerly anticipating his next world-building session with Matthew. However, as he sipped his coffee and read the news of the day, his phone rang. It was Matthew.

"Hey, Matthew! Looking forward to our session this afternoon," John said cheerfully.

"About that, John," Matthew began, "I'm going to be busy today. But I have an idea for Sunday. It's the last Sunday of the month, and I was thinking we could do something special."

John, slightly disappointed but curious, asked, "What do you have in mind?"

"How about we go for an Omakase at Longplay Hifi at noon?" Matthew suggested.

"Omakase? I've never heard of that," John replied, intrigued. "But I'm always up for new experiences."

"That's what I love about you, John," Matthew said with a smile in his voice. "Always open to trying something new."

"Where is this place?" John asked, pulling up his calendar to mark the date.

"It's at Imperial Ave," Matthew informed him.

"Got it. I'll see you on Sunday then," John said, already looking forward to the weekend.

Sunday arrived, and John drove to Longplay Hifi, following the directions on Google Maps. He arrived at the venue around 12:20 p.m., finding a spot in the cozy, eclectic neighborhood. The outside of the building was understated, but as John walked in, he was immediately drawn to the warmth and charm of the place.

Matthew was already seated at a long bar, waving him over with a grin. Behind the bar, shelves filled with vinyl records lined the walls, and classical music played softly in the background. John recognized the song instantly—it was "Blue in Green" by Miles Davis.

"Hey, John!" Matthew greeted him warmly as John took a seat next to him.

"Hi, Matthew! This place is amazing," John said, taking in the ambiance. "And this music—Miles Davis, right?"

"Yeah, one of my favorites," Matthew replied. "I thought you'd appreciate it."

John smiled. "You know me well. So, what exactly is Omakase?"

"It's a Japanese dining experience where the chef selects the dishes for you," Matthew explained. "You just sit back and enjoy."

"Oh," John said, feeling the excitement build. "Let's do this then."

As they settled in, the chef approached them, ready to guide them through a culinary adventure, and John couldn't wait to see what the day had in store.

John picked up the brochure that was placed in front of him, intrigued by its sleek design and inviting layout. He read: "LONGPLAY is a 'High-Fidelity Listening Club' dedicated to the promotion of audiophile culture, design, and hospitality."

John turned the page to reveal the menu featuring the dishes they would enjoy during their Omakase experience.

As they waited for the first course, Matthew turned to John with a thoughtful expression. "John, when you think about debt, how do you feel? Happy, sad, indifferent?"

John blinked, thinking, "I guess... mostly stressed. Why do you ask?"

Matthew pulled out a small pamphlet he had brought with him. "It's something I've been reading about. Here are some common emotions people express about debt of any type and amount: depression, anxiety, resentment, denial, stress, anger, frustration, regret, shame, embarrassment, fear."

John nodded slowly. "Yeah, I can relate to some of those."

"But as you look back," Matthew continued, "many of these emotions were absent while shopping or spending money. On the contrary, you may have felt excited, satisfied, and fulfilled during those moments."

"True," John admitted, thinking about past impulsive purchases. "Shopping can feel really good at the moment."

Matthew leaned forward, emphasizing his point. "Most of us can relate to these conditions. We all love to shop with credit but don't like the debt that follows. Consumer debt is the third cultural barrier to financial success."

John looked at him, intrigued. "So, what's your take on credit then?"

"The truth is that credit can be both good and bad, depending on several things," Matthew said. "Credit is a topic that is familiar to most people. If you're older than eighteen and live in an affluent country like the United States, you have access to credit. Presently, it is the most widely used method of spending money worldwide."

John nodded, understanding the importance of what Matthew was saying. "Yet despite its convenience, credit is the leading cause behind countless financial tragedies, especially in personal finance," Matthew continued. "For too many of us, credit has become a significant barrier to financial success. This is because it ravages cash reserves, enslaves borrowers, and potentially threatens insolvency when mismanaged."

"I see your point," John said thoughtfully. "So, what's the history behind it?"

"To see what I mean, we must step back in history," Matthew explained. "Before the 1700s, credit wasn't well-known in the US. Although the Pilgrims began using it in the mid-1600s, most people depended on cash to conduct business. But for many merchants, the cash system was too slow. They wanted a faster way to turn their inventory and make a profit."

"That makes sense," John said, leaning in.

"So, in the mid-1700s, they introduced installment credit to their customers, and it quickly became a popular way for some people to buy what they wanted. In a short time, the system paved the way for merchants to move their inventory and gave cash-poor people access to goods and services they couldn't obtain."

"It sounds like it helped a lot of people," John observed.

"In one way, yes," Matthew agreed. "But it had some limitations. Since credit catered to people in dire financial need, others refused to use it. They didn't want to be stigmatized as one with money problems...or worse, one without money."

"That's interesting," John said, contemplating the social aspects. "So how did they handle it?"

"Merchants kept credit transactions highly private," Matthew continued. "Butchers, cabinetmakers, grocers, and others kept credit dealings well documented and hidden from prying eyes. They were protecting the identity of their customers."

"That's quite considerate," John remarked.

"Meanwhile, installment credit was gaining popularity as more and more people began using the system. With installment loans, people borrow a set amount of money and repay the loan in monthly installments. The Annual Percentage Rate (APR) was fixed over the period. Once the balance was repaid, the account was closed."

Just then, a chef approached their table and placed a beautifully arranged dish in front of them. It was a delicate plate of sashimi, with thin slices of fresh tuna, salmon, and yellowtail, artfully garnished with edible flowers and a drizzle of soy reduction.

John tasted a piece, and his eyes lit up. "This is incredible," he said, looking up at the chef. "Thank you."

Matthew nodded in agreement, also savoring his first bite. "Yes, thank you. It's delicious."

The chef smiled and bowed slightly before returning to his station. Matthew and John exchanged appreciative glances, ready to dive deeper into both their culinary and intellectual explorations.

Matthew continued, taking small bites in between his words. "Today, people use installment loans to purchase everything from furniture and groceries to real estate.

The shame that was once associated with this system gradually dissipated. Unfortunately, as installment credit gained popularity, some people began to abuse it. They had difficulty honoring their contracts and ran into delinquency issues. Back then, merchants had little tolerance or sympathy for those who dishonored their credit agreements."

John, listening intently, nodded. "So what happened to those people?"

"Before the American Revolution, colony residents could be jailed for debt as small as fifty cents," Matthew said, pausing to sip his drink. "Debtors' prison was no fun. The rooms were small and usually crowded. Historical accounts describe them as horribly dirty and grossly nauseating, filled with fear, torture, torment, and even death."

John shuddered at the thought. "That's harsh. But the credit system still thrived?"

Matthew nodded. "Yes, it did. Some people had become hopelessly dependent on the system and saw no other way to survive, risking jail for credit delinquency. And it wasn't just the poorest affected. By the late 1700s, merchants developed a method to extend credit only to those who had the means to repay the debt, often affluent individuals. Even then, some defaulted and faced punishment."

He continued, "Charles Goodyear, the chemist who developed vulcanized rubber, was imprisoned for four days because he couldn't pay his debts. Robert Morris, one of the founding fathers, was also imprisoned for bad debt. During the American Revolution, George Washington depended on Morris for financial assistance. Morris borrowed against his assets to finance the war and provided the troops with clothing, food, supplies, and ammunition. Despite his significant contributions, he lacked self-discipline and good judgment over his finances, leading to his incarceration in 1798 for shady land deals."

"Wow," John said, leaning back. "And he was a founding father?"

"Yes," Matthew confirmed. "Later, he was released because of the National Bankruptcy Law passed in 1802. With bad health, a broken spirit, and evaporated assets, Robert Morris walked out of prison into poverty. Congress later remembered his contributions to the nation and pardoned him, placing his portrait on the 1880 ten-dollar bill as a token of appreciation."

John shook his head in disbelief. "That's quite a story."

"It is," Matthew agreed. "The system thrived despite the abuse of credit and the accompanying punishment. People resorted to credit to purchase what they wanted, especially with eye-popping inventions. In 1850, for example, millions of women became obsessed with the sewing machine. A shirt that took 15 hours to complete could now be done in one hour. With a $1 down payment and $4 monthly, Singer sold millions of $30 sewing machines on installment credit."

"That's incredible," John said, impressed.

"By the late 1900s, the shame associated with credit was completely gone," Matthew continued. "Eighty percent of all entertainment systems, seventy-five percent of laundry equipment, sixty-five percent of house-cleaning tools, and twenty-five percent of jewelry were bought on installment credit. Yet the system continued to entrap people who relied on it too heavily. Some went to debtors' prison, and others had their valuables repossessed."

Just then, another dish was placed in front of them. This time, it was a beautifully plated sushi roll garnished with fresh herbs and a delicate drizzle of sauce. John took a bite, and his eyes widened with delight. "This is fantastic. Never knew I had a thing for Japanese cuisine," he said, nodding to the chef.

Matthew smiled, savoring his own piece. "Yes, it's excellent."

After the chef bowed and left, Matthew continued, "Anyway, by 1920, more people were experiencing credit destruction. Those who hadn't gotten trapped by the system knew or heard about others who had. Credit seemed like a contradiction—allowing access to essential products and services without cash, yet many had difficulty repaying the debt."

"It created a financial nightmare for merchants and consumers alike," John said, piecing it together.

"Exactly," Matthew replied. "This led to other lending methods, eventually giving rise to long-term credit for houses, cars, boats, etc. In the early 1900s, commercial banks, mutual savings, and mortgage companies expanded their services to accommodate the growing needs of consumers."

John looked thoughtful. "So, credit has always been a double-edged sword."

Matthew nodded. "Indeed. However, with unregulated lending, the system imploded, which resulted in the Great Depression of the 1930s. This was the most prolonged, profound, and pervasive depression of the 20th century."

John listened intently, his curiosity piqued.

Matthew continued while finishing the second dish, savoring each bite. "With the pain of the Great Depression still very real, bankers only advanced credit to people with adequate collateral," Matthew explained. "But by the early 1940s, they reintroduced long-term credit to consumers. The terms were concise. Homes and vehicle loans lasted no more than twelve months. Local butchers and grocers did something similar, giving credit only to people they trusted."

John took a sip of his drink, thinking about how strict those conditions must have been.

"All the same, the cautious approach to lending didn't last," Matthew continued. "After World War II, the country faced an extraordinary challenge. Millions of veterans returned home wanting jobs, education, and housing. But bankers were still reluctant to advance loans without collateral."

"So, what changed?" John asked.

"The government stepped in," Matthew said. "Congress passed the Servicemen's Readjustment Act of 1944, also known as the GI Bill. It allowed banks to extend credit for housing and education for millions of military personnel. With the federal government guaranteeing loans, millions of veterans took advantage of the opportunity. They purchased homes, paid for education, and went into business. Later, the program was expanded to include nonmilitary personnel, which created a credit boom in the country."

John leaned forward, clearly fascinated. "That must have had a huge impact."

"It did," Matthew replied. "The collaboration between the government and the private sector was good for the economy at the time. It relaxed lenders' tight grip on money, and people regained their confidence in the credit system. As a result, demand for goods and services increased, and the economy proliferated. The changes were felt around the world. But with the rise of credit usage, the delinquency rate also skyrocketed. Banks reacted by implementing more stringent borrowing criteria, which threatened to stifle the economy once again."

John shook his head. "It sounds like a rollercoaster."

"It was," Matthew agreed. "The construction, automobile, and appliance industries were affected. The real estate market was also unstable. Despite that, the economy continued sluggishly for several years until the early sixties. Then, a new group of young bankers, who had no ties to the Great Depression, relaxed the lending rules. By the mid-1970s, Americans had regained their faith in the credit system."

John smiled, starting to see the broader picture. "So, that's when revolving credit came into play?"

"Yes," Matthew confirmed. "Revolving credit is an open account that allows you to withdraw funds, repay them, and withdraw them again. It is the most popular credit system today. No one knows for sure how it began, but the best estimate is around 1951 when Franklin National Bank released its first credit card. Because of its flexibility, revolving credit has become the leading choice by which most people conduct business today."

John nodded. "It seems like credit has a long and complex history."

"Indeed," Matthew said, taking another bite. "Despite the long history of credit, the system hasn't changed that much. Many of the old methods of borrowing money are still in place. Financial institutions have just developed more sophisticated ways to package money for consumers. Like the generations before us, we like using credit. Since few of us have cash, credit is our primary way of spending money. This means that millions of us depend on the system daily to buy everything we want."

"But credit can be dangerous," John remarked.

"Absolutely," Matthew replied. "Credit has remained true to its nature. Like a venomous snake, its deadly sting is always present. Each year, millions of people fall prey to its bite. This is due to several reasons, among them a lack of understanding of credit. Today's younger generations are confused about the system. Credit gives them access to money, but they have no idea who owns it. Most don't know if the money belongs to them, the bank, or investors. A large majority of people believe that the money they borrow through credit belongs to them."

John looked puzzled. "But it doesn't, right?"

"No," Matthew said, shaking his head. "And herein lies part of the problem with credit. We believe we've earned the money and have the right to use it. This belief is more widespread than you realize, especially among younger people. But this thinking is dangerous. It gets a ton of people into financial trouble each year. The tendency is to keep shopping as long as credit is available on the account. At the same time, we react differently to cash. We are more cautious about parting with a dollar."

"Why is that?" John asked.

"We subconsciously perceive cash to have more value than credit," Matthew explained. "For most of us, shopping is a fun activity. And with credit, entertainment goes up a few notches because of the temporary freedom to spend without limits. Slogans such as 'Get cash back on every purchase,' 'You deserve it,' and 'Buy now and save' appeal to our emotions and keep us running to the malls daily to buy things on credit."

John leaned back, taking in all the information. "I see what you mean."

Matthew smiled, seeing the realization in John's eyes. "Yes, understanding credit is very important. It can be a powerful tool if used wisely, but it can also lead to financial ruin if mismanaged."

As they continued their conversation, another dish arrived, this time a beautifully prepared plate of tempura vegetables, crisp and golden. They both appreciated the artistry and flavors, savoring the meal while reflecting on the complex and nuanced history of credit.

Matthew continued, his tone growing more serious, "But debt is no funny business. It hurts people, destroys families, and turns credit abusers into second-grade citizens because of distrust. When things go wrong with credit abusers, they are placed in a subprime category for excessively high interest rates. And even then, many of them can't stop spending. So, they keep borrowing until their financial system collapses entirely."

John nodded, recognizing the truth in Matthew's words. "It's like a never-ending cycle," he commented.

"Exactly," Matthew agreed, taking a small bite of the third dish that had just arrived. "Others tend to ignore the debt aspect of credit during the shopping spree. The reality of credit occurs only when the bill comes due. It is only then that we feel the financial impact of our decision. By then, the impulse that led to the purchase had dissipated. What's left is the debt – the money owed for the purchased items."

John sighed, recalling his own experiences with credit card bills. "It's a harsh wake-up call."

Matthew nodded. "And this is when we begin to feel some of the negative emotions mentioned at the beginning: depression, regret, shame, etc. The invitation to use credit for personal gain sounds like a great idea initially. You can use the money anywhere for anything. But you must use the funds before you have debt. When you use it, you owe the lender a debt obligation. At that point, the relationship between you and the lender changes...legally. The agreement binds you until the debt is paid in full. At which point do you become an indentured servant?"

John raised his eyebrows, surprised by the blunt term.

"In this arrangement, you're immediately placed at a financial disadvantage," Matthew explained. "Believe it or not, this is where the lender wants you to be. Since you're legally bound to repay the debt, the lender sees you as a profit center. Each month, you'll pay a portion of the principal and interest due on the balance. The interest portion will be the lender's profits."

John frowned. "So, it's in their best interest to keep us in debt?"

"Exactly," Matthew said. "To gain more interest, the lender will send you periodic invitations to spend more money. Part of the invitation will sometimes include incentives such as cashback on purchases, travel miles, etc. The hope is that you will run to the store and buy more things. The higher your balance, the greater the interest on the amount due, which the lender wants."

"Who benefits more from your credit purchases: you or the lender?" Matthew asked, looking John in the eye.

"The lender," John replied slowly.

"Right," Matthew confirmed. "Your purchase may have some value, often temporary. But the lender derives more excellent value from the transaction. The one who collects the interest payment is the financial winner. The higher the balance, the longer it takes to repay the debt and the more profit the lender collects from you. This means you'll pay much interest if you have two or three credit accounts with high balances. Often, it takes years to pay off these balances. Meanwhile, the lender will get richer because of your payments."

John sighed again, feeling the weight of Matthew's words.

"So, from a business standpoint, lenders need to flood the market with money through credit," Matthew continued. "This explains the ongoing war with American Express, MasterCard, Visa, and Discover. They all compete for a large pool of customers. The one with the most customers will likely make the most money. This is because every consumer is a source of profit."

John shook his head. "The whole system is designed to keep us trapped."

"That's precisely true. The whole credit system favors the rich," Matthew said. "Picture a small number of wealthy people who control most of the money in the world. They invest their money with banks and mortgage companies that lend to a larger group of cash-poor people who want to buy things—cars, boats, houses, etc. They charge a fee (interest) for the privilege to use the money. When the cycle is complete, they are more affluent, and those who owe them are poorer."

John looked thoughtful. "So, the only way to beat the system is to stop using credit?"

Matthew smiled. "That's one way, but it's not likely to happen any time soon. The next best thing is to become a lender, which is what I'm hoping for you. That way, you'll be collecting interest instead of paying interest. This is where your money would be making money... for you."

John's eyes widened. "That sounds like a much better position to be in."

"At the same time, remember that credit isn't entirely bad," Matthew said. "Many people have used the system to prosper. They borrowed money for business and succeeded. This type of situation will continue to happen. Credit is beneficial for people who venture into business for profit. But sadly, it's not the same for consumers. Most people use credit for everyday spending, which is not profitable. The system eventually traps them."

"Though few people go to debtors' prison these days, many have come close to spending time in jail," Matthew added. "Thank goodness for bankruptcy protection. Each year, many people file bankruptcy petitions. Millions more are struggling to keep their heads above water. Knowing this, I hope you can see how debt can be a significant barrier to financial independence."

John nodded slowly. "It's a constant drain on resources."

"Along with other expenses, the balance owed continually drains cash resources," Matthew emphasized. "Much of this money could easily be put into a profitable venture that could make you wealthy."

Just then, the chef brought out something sweet—a beautifully presented plate of matcha green tea ice cream with a drizzle of honey and fresh berries. The colors and delicate flavors offered a delightful end to their meal. Matthew and John each took a spoonful of the matcha green tea ice cream and literally yummed. The rich, creamy texture blended perfectly with the subtle bitterness of the matcha and the sweetness of the honey and fresh berries. They savored the delicious treat, exchanging satisfied glances as the chef left them to enjoy their dessert in peace.

Matthew, feeling both content and focused, continued, "Now, what I would recommend is, because of how our culture is set up, I don't suggest getting rid of credit entirely. Credit is a valuable tool. Without it, our economic system would come to a crawl, and some businesses would stagnate and fail."

John nodded thoughtfully, licking his spoon clean. "Yeah, I can see that. It's kind of ingrained in everything we do."

"Exactly," Matthew agreed. "Besides, most establishments won't conduct business with you without a significant credit card. Car rental companies, hotels, and many other businesses expect you to have one for use. So, having an active credit account is essential. The idea is to use it – if you must – but avoid accumulating debt. The debt is the trap. Often, it takes years to pay off the balance owed. Meanwhile, you hope your income remains steady or grows to meet the demanding debt obligation."

John leaned forward, absorbing Matthew's advice. "So, how do you manage it without falling into the trap?"

Matthew smiled, appreciating John's eagerness to learn. "To minimize debt conflict, consider doing the following: Control your impulses for buying things. The more you spend, the poorer you become."

John chuckled. "Easier said than done, but I get it."

"True," Matthew acknowledged. "But it's crucial. If you have credit balances, pay them off quickly. Use a trusted debt consolidation agency to help you. Put some money away while paying off your debt. This way, you'll make progress on two fronts."

John's eyes widened with understanding. "So, I should save and pay off debt at the same time?"

"Exactly," Matthew said. "Limit your credit cards to one... no more than two. The more open credit accounts you have, the more you'll likely get into financial trouble. If you must borrow money, attempt to pay off the balance in full. This will minimize interest charges and prevent delinquency. Above all, avoid using your savings to pay off debt. Hold onto your cash while paying off the balance owed."

John nodded, making mental notes. "That makes a lot of sense. It's about balance and discipline."

"Precisely," Matthew confirmed, finishing his ice cream. "Credit can be your friend if you use it wisely. It's not about avoiding it altogether but managing it so that it doesn't manage you."

John took another spoonful, savoring the flavors while pondering Matthew's words. "Thanks, Matthew. I feel like I have a clearer picture now."

Matthew smiled warmly. "I'm glad to hear that. Remember, the goal is financial independence and managing credit is just one step on that journey."

As the plates were cleared and the last remnants of their delightful meal were savored, Matthew glanced at his watch. "Well, John, I think it's time for us to head out," he said, pushing back his chair and standing up.

John followed suit, rising from his seat and stretching a bit. "Yeah, you're right. This was really informative, Matthew. Thanks for all the insights."

Matthew grinned, extending his hand. "Anytime, John. It's always a pleasure to share what I know, and I'm glad you're finding it useful."

They shook hands firmly, a gesture that solidified not only their conversation but also their friendship. "We'll definitely have to meet up for our next session," John said enthusiastically.

Matthew's eyes twinkled with a hint of mischief as he winked. "And trust me, there will be more surprises."

John chuckled, a broad smile spreading across his face. "I'm looking forward to it."

They walked towards the entrance of Longplay Hifi, the sounds of vinyl records still playing softly in the background. As they stepped outside, the warm afternoon sun greeted them. They bid each other farewell, John heading towards his car and Matthew walking down the street, their minds both buzzing with thoughts of credit, debt, and the intriguing world of finance.

"Take care, John!" Matthew called over his shoulder.

"You too, Matthew! See you soon!" John replied, waving as he opened his car door.

As John drove away, he felt anticipated for their next meeting. Matthew's promise of surprise left him curious and excited for what was to come.

CHAPTER 13

❦

A Closer Look at Taxes and Wealth

The sun began to set, casting a warm, golden glow over Balboa Park. The park was alive with color, and the gardens flourished under the summer sky. The Inez Grant Parker Memorial Rose Garden, in particular, was in a riot of reds, pinks, yellows, and whites, the roses in full bloom. The scent of the flowers hung in the air, mingling with the earthy smell of freshly watered soil. The gentle sound of water splashing from the Bea Evenson Fountain nearby provided a soothing background to their wealth-building session. People were scattered across the park, some taking leisurely strolls, others sitting on benches, admiring the view.

Matthew and John walked slowly, their pace matching the relaxed rhythm of the evening. The roses surrounded them, their petals soft and delicate, catching the last light of the day. Matthew gently brushed his fingers against a nearby bloom, feeling the smooth texture of the petals.

"Sometimes being in touch with nature is necessary," Matthew mused, breaking the comfortable silence between them. He turned to John, his gaze thoughtful.

"It's important to remind ourselves that we're part of something bigger. We get so caught up in the hustle of life, in chasing financial goals, that we forget...this." He gestured to the garden around them, a soft smile on his face. "Nature doesn't rush, but everything gets done in its own time."

John nodded, taking in the serene beauty of the garden. "You're right. It's easy to forget the simple things, especially when we're trying to build something more for ourselves."

They walked on in silence for a few moments, each lost in their thoughts. The path curved gently, leading them toward a secluded bench under a canopy of trees. The bench was slightly worn, and the wood was polished smoothly from years of use. They sat down, the sound of birds chirping softly in the distance.

After a pause, Matthew leaned back, his expression serious. "So far, you've discovered three major cultural hindrances to financial independence," he began, his tone shifting to a more instructive one. "These are hurdles that many people face, often without even realizing it."

John leaned, listening intently as Matthew continued. "First, there's growing up financially illiterate. It's a problem that starts in childhood and extends into adulthood. Schools teach us how to read and write, but they don't teach us how to manage money. So, we end up learning the hard way, often making mistakes that could have been avoided."

Matthew glanced at John, making sure he was following. "Then there's the issue of obtaining a college degree through credit. Most people depend on student loans to pay for school, and they begin their adult life with a considerable debt hanging over their heads. It takes years to repay, and during that time, financial independence remains out of reach."

John nodded thoughtfully, reflecting on his own experiences. "I've seen that happen to so many people," he said quietly. "It's like they start life on the back foot, always trying to catch up."

Matthew continued, his voice steady. "The third hindrance is a credit system that preys on the financially disadvantaged. The rich lend money to those who can least afford it, charging steep interest rates. In the process, the rich get richer, and the borrowers sink deeper into debt. These are conditions that, to some degree, individuals can manage—they can choose to accept or decline them."

John frowned, "But what about things we can't control? Like taxes?"

Matthew smiled, "Exactly. Taxes on income are controlled by state and federal governments. Lawmakers make the rules, and we abide by them. If we don't, we get penalized. So, we have no choice but to find ways to minimize our tax obligations, which we'll discuss toward the end of this module."

He paused, letting the information sink in. "Can the government hinder your financial progress? Yes, it can. It's happening every day. Taxes on income are the fourth cultural barrier to financial success. Think of it this way: what is your most significant work incentive?"

"The money," John replied without hesitation.

Matthew nodded. "Exactly. Though you derive other benefits from your job—like contributing to society, job satisfaction, and so on—money takes precedence. At the end of the day, the paycheck is everything. But just as badly as you need the money, the government wants it even more."

John's eyes narrowed as he considered this. "So, it's like we're in a constant tug-of-war over our income."

"Yes," Matthew agreed. "You and the government are at odds over your income. The objective is to determine who gets to keep more of it. Over the years, lawmakers have become highly crafty in reaching into people's pocketbooks. They manipulate the tax laws to confuse the public, making it difficult to determine how much you pay each year."

He leaned in slightly, his voice low and serious. "To date, people in this nation work roughly four months a year just to pay federal, state, and local taxes. Tax Freedom Day usually falls in April, marking the day when Americans have earned enough money to pay their tax obligations to the government. The amount is usually in the trillions of dollars each year, and your tax contribution is part of that sum."

John let out a low whistle. "That's a lot of money."

"It is," Matthew agreed. "And the government knows better than to take it all at once. If they left you without money for a prolonged period, you would scream, and the system wouldn't work as well. So, they use a nibbling approach, taking the funds in stages. That way, most people don't even notice the incremental losses."

Matthew's expression softened slightly as he continued. "If you habitually get a refund at the end of each year, it means the government is withholding too much of your money. You might get excited about the refund check, but you lost some opportunities in the process. You didn't have access to the funds for financial gains, and the government paid you no interest on the withholding."

John sighed, "And then we spend the entire amount as soon as we get it, right? That's what most people do."

Matthew nodded. "Exactly. So, economically, you make no financial headway with the refund, leaving you in the same condition as last year. It's a cycle that keeps people from achieving true financial independence."

The two men sat in silence for a moment, the sounds of the park fading into the background as they absorbed the significance of their conversation. The sky above had deepened to a rich indigo, the first stars beginning to twinkle in the evening light. The world around them felt distant, as if the only thing that mattered was the truth they had uncovered.

Finally, John broke the silence. "So, what's the next step? How do we break free from these barriers?"

"John, to really understand where we are today with taxes, it's important to look back at how it all began. The origin of income tax in America is tied deeply to the country's history, and it's been a long and winding road to where we are now."

John's interest was piqued. "I know a little bit about taxes but not much about how it all started. I'm curious—what led to the creation of income tax in the first place?"

Matthew nodded, appreciating John's curiosity. "The idea of income tax in America first emerged out of necessity. It all began during the American Civil War in 1861. The government needed funds to support the war effort, and they decided to introduce an income tax as a way to raise that money. At the time, the tax rate was quite modest—3% on income over $800 a year."

John raised an eyebrow. "That sounds low compared to today's standards. What happened next?"

Matthew continued, "In 1862, with the war still raging and costs mounting, the government decided to increase the tax rate. They raised it to 5% on income over $10,000 a year. This was a significant increase and broadened the tax base, allowing the government to collect more revenue."

John nodded slowly, following the timeline. "So, it was all about funding the war?"

"Exactly," Matthew replied. "But once the war ended, people became concerned about the continuation of these taxes. The prevailing attitude was 'no war, no taxes.' To them, taxation without a pressing cause seemed unethical—a direct violation of personal freedom."

John's brow furrowed as he considered this. "It makes sense. If there's no need for it, why keep it?"

Matthew smiled slightly, recognizing the sentiment. "That was exactly the public's argument. However, despite the public outcry, Congress chose to ignore their plea. The government continued to collect taxes, even without the justification of war. This led to growing discontent, and the issue of balancing the budget became a significant challenge. Income tax and revenue from tariffs weren't enough to cover the government's expenses."

John frowned, intrigued by the historical context. "So, what did the government do?"

"In 1893," Matthew explained, "Congress passed laws making income tax the primary source of revenue. But in 1895, the Supreme Court ruled that the practice was unconstitutional. This ruling threw the government's plans into disarray."

John's eyes widened slightly. "Unconstitutional? How did they justify collecting taxes after that?"

"That's where President William Howard Taft came in," Matthew said, his tone growing more intense. "He introduced the Sixteenth Amendment to the Constitution, which made it lawful to collect tax on personal income. In 1913, this amendment was ratified, making income tax legally binding. Since then, it has become a permanent fixture in American life."

John shook his head, impressed by the twists and turns of history. "It's amazing how something that started as a temporary measure for war funding became such a fundamental part of our system."

"It is," Matthew agreed. "And over the years, lawmakers have become highly creative with tax laws. When the government's budget gets out of control, they raise the tax rate to accommodate the change. If existing laws don't allow for it, they create new ones to serve the same purpose. For instance, during World War II, federal spending skyrocketed, and to keep up, the tax rate was increased significantly. The tax base also expanded from 14 million to 50 million taxpayers."

John's expression turned serious as he processed the information. "So, it's a constant cycle of spending and taxing?"

"Exactly," Matthew confirmed. "Since 1943, lawmakers have made more than 30 different revisions to tax laws. Some of these changes have lasted no more than a year. It's a reflection of the government's ongoing struggle to balance its budget while managing its spending. For example, between 1993 and 2001, there were five tax brackets, but in 2001, Congress created another one, raising it to six brackets. Each change is an attempt to generate additional revenue as the government continues to overspend."

John took a deep breath, realizing the complexity of the issue. "So, whenever there's a budget shortfall, personal income becomes the target?"

"Unfortunately, yes," Matthew said with a nod. "Personal income often becomes the primary target for additional revenue. Most people don't realize it, but there are two main types of taxes on income. The first is what we call front-end taxes. This is the portion of your money that's taken out of your gross income each payday. It's broken down into smaller, identifiable lots—federal tax, state tax, Social Security, Medicare, and so on."

John's eyes narrowed slightly as he considered the implications. "That's the money I see disappearing from my paycheck every month."

"Exactly," Matthew replied. "Your tax rate, which is based on the total amount of tax divided by your income, determines your withholding and tax obligation. This rate can vary depending on your income, and while it's fixed for now, it's subject to change in the future, often depending on the whims of Congress. We can only hope that future changes will lower the rate, allowing you to keep more of your hard-earned money."

John nodded, his mind racing with thoughts about his own finances. "But with all these different types of taxes, how much of the government's revenue actually comes from income tax?"

Matthew's expression grew more serious as he answered. "To date, state and federal governments collect tax revenue from various sources—corporate tax, excise tax, property tax, estate tax, gift tax, and capital gains tax, to name a few. However, income tax makes up a significant portion of their revenue. It's the backbone of the government's income, and unfortunately, this ratio is not likely to change in the future. If anything, it's likely to increase as the government looks for more ways to fund its spending."

John sighed, "So, no matter what, it seems like we're always going to be dealing with these taxes."

Matthew offered a sympathetic smile. "It's a challenging reality, but understanding how it all works gives you the power to navigate it more effectively. The key is to stay informed, plan strategically, and take control of what you can. That way, you can minimize the impact of taxes on your financial goals and move closer to financial independence."

John took a deep breath, feeling both the burden and the empowerment that comes with knowledge. "Thanks, Matthew. I've got a lot to think about."

Matthew nodded, his eyes full of encouragement. "You're on the right path, John. Keep asking questions, keep learning, and don't let the complexity of the system deter you. We're in this together, and with the right approach, you can achieve the financial freedom you're aiming for."

Matthew and John found themselves standing in front of a small café that overlooked the park.

"How about a warm drink?" Matthew asked John.

"Sure," John nodded.

The interior was warm, with wooden furniture and soft lighting creating a comfortable atmosphere. A few other patrons were scattered around, quietly sipping their drinks and chatting. The soft hum of conversation mixed with the sound of the espresso machine added to the relaxed ambiance. The windows of the café offered a view of the park, now faintly lit under the evening sky. A light drizzle started outside, pattering softly against the windows, adding a soothing rhythm to the background. As the waitress approached, Matthew and John glanced at the menu briefly before placing their orders. Matthew ordered his usual—black coffee, strong and straightforward. John, opting for something with a bit more comfort, requested a latte. The waitress nodded, jotting down their choices before heading back to the counter.

Matthew leaned back in his chair, folding his hands over his stomach, a contemplative expression on his face. "John, there's something you need to understand about government spending and how it affects your financial future," he began, his tone serious. "Government spending isn't just a temporary issue; it's something that will most likely continue to rise over time. And as it does, you can expect that taxpayers like us will have less disposable income to work with in the future."

John furrows his brow, listening intently. "So, you're saying that the more the government spends, the more they'll take from us?"

Matthew nods, his gaze steady. "Exactly. Lawmakers will always find a way to take more money from your income, even if it means creating new taxes or raising existing ones. Historically, that's the way things have always been done. But what most people don't realize is how these tax increases directly affect our lives."

He paused as the waitress returned with their drinks, setting down the steaming cups on the table. John wrapped his hands around his latte, savoring the warmth, while Matthew took a small sip of his black coffee.

"The truth is," Matthew continued, setting his cup down, "each incremental tax increase leaves us with less money to save or spend. And when you have less disposable income, it becomes much harder to get ahead financially."

John nodded slowly, mulling over the implications. "I guess I've always just accepted taxes as a part of life. I never really thought about how much they take from what I earn."

"That's part of the problem," Matthew says, leaning in slightly. "We've all been conditioned to accept these front-end taxes, the ones that are clearly defined and itemized on your pay statement. You see exactly how much is being taken out for federal tax, state tax, Social Security, Medicare, and all the rest. But there's another type of income tax that's far more deceptive—back-end taxes."

John looked up, intrigued. "Back-end taxes? What do you mean by that?"

Matthew took another sip of his coffee before answering. "Back-end taxes are the taxes you pay without even realizing it, often when you're doing everyday things like shopping or paying bills. For example, after you've already paid roughly 15% of your income in taxes from your paycheck, you might think you're done with your tax obligations for the month. But that's not entirely true."

He leaned forward, emphasizing his next point. "The remaining 85% of your take-home pay is still the target of additional taxes. This is the part most people don't see until that portion of their money is gone. Every time you buy something, you're paying sales tax. And in some places, that adds up quickly."

John's eyes widened slightly as he began to connect the dots. "So, even after paying income tax, I'm still losing money through these hidden taxes."

"Exactly," Matthew confirmed. "Take Texas, for example. The state has a base sales tax, but local jurisdictions can add their own tax on top of that, raising the total amount. So, every time you buy something— whether it's a house, a car, gasoline, or even clothing— you're paying that combined sales tax."

John shook his head, the reality of it sinking in. "That's a lot more than I realized. And I guess it's not just sales tax, either."

"No, it's not," Matthew agreed. "And the thing is, sales taxes rarely go down. Government spending tends to rise, and when lawmakers can't hike the tax rate directly, they find other ways to get the money they need. They might pass new laws or regulations that establish or increase existing fees on properties, roads, transportation, gasoline, and other necessities."

He took another sip of his coffee before continuing. "Whether it's sales taxes or these other fees, the effect is the same—they're all back-end taxes designed to reach into your pocket and leave you with less money for your personal needs. The goal, as always, is to siphon off your hard-earned income into government treasuries."

John let out a slow breath, feeling a bit overwhelmed. "It's like no matter what I do, the government is always taking a cut."

Matthew nodded sympathetically. "It feels that way because it's true. Besides payroll taxes, sales taxes, and various government fees attached to transactions, you also have to pay property taxes if you own a home. This is an annual government requirement, and the amount you pay each year depends on your home's value. The rate varies depending on the state, but it can range from very low to quite high. In Texas, for instance, the rate is somewhere in the middle."

John's frown deepened. "That's a lot of money, especially when you add it all up."

"It is," Matthew agreed. "The actual dollar amount for the average family can vary between $1,000 and $10,000 a year, just for property tax. And that's in addition to all the other taxes you've already paid. So, if you take the time to calculate your annual front-end and back-end taxes, including fees and property taxes, the total amount you pay each year would likely surprise you."

John raised an eyebrow. "How much are we talking about?"

"A rough estimate would put it close to 0.35 cents on the dollar," Matthew said. "That means you're left with roughly 0.65 cents for savings, debt payments, and other essential items. This partly explains why so many people depend on their credit cards to make ends meet. The remaining cash from their paycheck can only stretch so far."

John sighed, "No wonder so many people are struggling financially."

"Exactly,' Matthew said, his voice tinged with frustration. "And yet, politicians continue to scheme behind closed doors to take even more money from taxpayers' pockets. These days, unfortunately, lawmakers feel they can tax us at will, even without our voting consent. The tax system is incredibly complex, and most people don't understand it. We feel helpless against politicians and their plans."

John looked down at his latte, his thoughts racing. "So, we're just being taken advantage of."

"That's exactly how they envision the situation," Matthew said, his tone growing sharper. "The more confused we are about the system, the easier it is for them to rob us in daylight. This allows them to push their agenda forward with minimal interruption."

He paused, allowing John to absorb the information before continuing. "John, if you haven't given much thought to taxes on income until now, think of it this way: The higher the tax rate, the more money you'll pay in taxes. The more you pay in taxes, the less money you'll have to achieve your financial goals. It doesn't matter what entity is collecting the taxes—whether it's the local, state, or federal government. The result of front-end or back-end taxes is the same: You're paying them with the same income you need for saving and spending."

John leaned back in his chair, rubbing his temples as he tried to process everything. "So, if I can't find enough money to advance my financial goals, it's because the government is taking a good portion of it."

Matthew nodded solemnly. "Exactly. Like the cultural hindrances we talked about earlier, income tax leaves you with less disposable income for financial progress. And as always, making more money— whether it's yours or someone else's—requires money. If you have little or none of it, getting ahead financially becomes much more complicated."

He continued, "When some of your income goes into government treasuries each month, it's hard to find the financial resources to ramp up your dreams unless you can borrow it, which presents a whole new set of challenges. But here's the harsh truth, John—if you can't achieve your financial dreams because of a lack of money, it's unlikely that politicians will care."

John looked up, meeting Matthew's eyes with a troubled expression. "It seems that way."

"Even more troubling is," Matthew continued, "If you're needy, homeless, or hungry, your condition would be of little consequence to lawmakers. Worse still, the Internal Revenue Service, the IRS, won't make your life any easier if you can't pay your tax obligation. They're notorious for being ruthless with those who can't pay their taxes. People who are delinquent on their taxes have had their bank accounts seized, homes sold, and businesses shut down by the IRS."

John shook his head, feeling a sense of dread. "That's terrifying."

"It is," Matthew agreed. But before we end this conversation, I want to make one thing clear—I'm not opposed to paying taxes. All through my life, I've filed my income tax return early, and I take pride in doing that—knowing that, to the best of my knowledge, I owe the government no back taxes."

Matthew took a slow sip of his black coffee, the bitterness grounding him as he looked across the table at John. He paused, letting his words sink in, then leaned forward slightly. "I strongly suggest that you develop a similar habit, John. Filing on time, keeping everything in order—it's more than just good practice. It prevents any unnecessary confrontation with the IRS. Trust me, you don't want to be on their bad side."

John nodded again, this time more thoughtfully. "I get that, Matthew. But it's tough, you know? The system feels so overwhelming at times."

"It does," Matthew agreed, his eyes softening with understanding. "But it's a necessary evil, isn't it? Our federal, state, and local governments need money to fund essential functions. The military, law enforcement, the National Guard, schools, roads, highways, and so many other vital services—these are things we all rely on."

John could see the conviction in Matthew's eyes. There was a deep-seated belief in the necessity of these systems despite their flaws. But he also knew that Matthew wasn't one to accept things without question blindly.

"The issue," Matthew continued, his voice growing firmer, "is not whether one should or shouldn't pay taxes. It's about the excessive tax that the government draws each year from the very people who are struggling to get ahead in life. We pay into a system that sometimes feels like it's working against us."

His gaze drifted out the window to the garden beyond, "Based on how frequently our government overspends, some politicians disregard spending limits. And why? Because the money feels free to them. As such, they squander it on swelling budgets and put the financial burden on the public."

John shifted in his seat, "It's the middle class, isn't it? We're the ones who carry the brunt of it."

"Exactly," Matthew replied, his gaze snapping back to meet John's. "The middle class is always hit the hardest. They struggle to survive, and yet they're the ones expected to shoulder the biggest share of the tax burden."

John frowned, stirring his latte absently. "But why? What's the motive behind all these tax increases?"

"That's the thing," Matthew said, "The motive is often unclear. The government can say one thing and do something completely different. And to make matters worse, they often refuse to let the public vote on a tax increase. Too often, these decisions are made behind closed doors, without our input or consent."

There was a moment of silence as both men sat with their thoughts. The café's ambient noise filled the space between them, a stark contrast to the heavy topic they were discussing.

Finally, Matthew sighed, taking another sip of his coffee. "It's a complex system, John, one that feels impossible to navigate at times. But understanding it, being aware of how it affects us—that's the first step toward taking control of our financial futures."

John nodded slowly, absorbing everything Matthew had said. The weight of the conversation pressed on him, and he leaned back in his chair, staring into the depths of his now half-empty latte. "So, what should one do?" he asked.

Matthew met John's gaze, his expression serious but calm. "There's little you can do to stop a tax increase, especially when you're denied the opportunity to vote on it. Once the law is passed, you're obligated to comply to avoid even more complications."

John's brow furrowed as he considered Matthew's words. "But can't people protest? Make their voices heard?"

Matthew nodded, acknowledging the point. "Certainly, you can protest the increase, but often, that carries little traction. Protests can raise awareness, but they rarely overturn laws. The government tends to move forward regardless, especially if it's convinced that the tax hike is necessary. So, while protesting has its place, you also need to remain vigilant."

"Vigilant?" John repeated, curiosity edging into his voice.

"Yes," Matthew replied, his eyes locking with John's. "Stay informed. Keep an eye on any proposed tax increases. The next time a politician talks about raising taxes on the rich, be cautious. It might sound good on the surface, but historically, changes to tax laws in the United States mostly affect the middle class."

John's confusion deepened. "But isn't the tax hike supposed to target the wealthy?"

"That's what they say," Matthew replied with a knowing sigh. "But in reality, the middle class—those earning between $50,000 to $150,000 a year—often end up shouldering the burden. The wealthy have ways to minimize their tax liabilities, ways that the average person doesn't have access to."

John frowned, realizing the implications. "So, by supporting these tax hikes, we're actually hurting ourselves?"

"Exactly," Matthew confirmed, "An increase in taxes means less money in your pocket. And that can affect your ability to save, invest, or even cover basic expenses. It's a chain reaction: higher taxes lead to reduced disposable income, which then limits your financial growth."

John took a deep breath, the weight of the conversation settling in. "So, if given the chance to vote on a tax increase…?"

"Vote 'NO,'" Matthew said without hesitation. "Of course, it's ultimately your decision, but if your goal is to improve your financial well-being, a tax hike is counterproductive. The pennies you pay to the government might seem small, but when you add them up across the population, they become billions of dollars for the treasury—and less for you."

He paused, letting John process the information. "By voting 'No,' you're not just expressing your opposition to the increase; you're sending a message to politicians that you won't accept having more of your hard-earned income siphoned away."

John nodded slowly, understanding the gravity of the situation. "But what if people just accept it? What if they're too complacent?"

Matthew's expression grew more intense as he leaned in closer. "There's a lesson to be learned from the Boston Tea Party. Remember, it was a political protest on December 16, 1773, in Boston. American colonists were fed up with Britain's 'taxation without representation.' They dumped 342 chests of tea into the harbor in defiance."

John's eyes widened as he recalled the history lesson. "And Britain eventually repealed the taxes, right?"

"Most of them, yes," Matthew affirmed. "But they kept the tea tax because they wanted the revenue from the millions of pounds of tea the colonists drank each year. In response, the colonists boycotted the tea from the British East India Company and smuggled tea from other countries instead."

John leaned back, connecting the dots. "So, by taking a stand, they hit Britain where it hurt—economically."

"Exactly," Matthew said with a satisfied nod. "The British East India Company was left with millions of pounds of unsold tea and faced bankruptcy. The colonists' protest wasn't just about making noise; it was about strategic resistance."

John stared into his latte, feeling the weight of history and its relevance to today. "So, you're saying we need to be strategic in how we respond to these tax increases?"

Matthew smiled, a hint of pride in his expression. "That's right. Being informed, staying vigilant, and making your voice heard through your vote through powerful tools. Your financial future depends on it."

John sat back, the gravity of the conversation settling in. The world seemed a little clearer, the challenges a little more defined. As they finished their coffee, John realized that the conversation had changed his perspective — not just on taxes, but on how he approached his financial life in general.

CHAPTER 14

✎✎✎

The Biggest Cash Flow Mistake

John and Matthew arrived at San Diego SeaWorld just as the gates opened. The sun was climbing over the horizon, spreading across the sprawling park. Families with excited children hurried ahead as their laughter mingled with the splashes and calls of marine animals. The two men walked, soaking in the early morning atmosphere.

As they strolled past the otter enclosure, John watched the creatures dart through the water, their sleek bodies twisting and turning with an effortless grace. "Look at them go," John remarked with a subtle smile, "Someone's having fun."

Matthew nodded thoughtfully, gazing at the otters. "They are, in a way. But they're also in a controlled environment. Their freedom and fun are limited to the space they're given."

John considered this for a moment before responding, "Kind of like the housing market, isn't it? We think we have freedom, but our choices are often dictated by external factors."

Matthew chuckled, "Exactly. Speaking of which, real estate has been and will continue to be an excellent vehicle for wealth creation. Investors who understand the housing market can purchase properties at auction prices and sell them for thousands of dollars over cost. They can buy foreclosure properties and turn them for huge profits. Even rundown properties, with a little bit of fixing, can be sold for a considerable gain."

They made their way to the aquarium, where the cool, faint light had a calming effect on their eyes. As they walked through the tunnel, surrounded by the serene, flowing motion of various fish and marine life, Matthew began to share his thoughts.

John nodded as he watched a school of fish swim by. "So you're saying there's a lot of potential out there, but only if you know what you're doing."

"Precisely," Matthew replied, his eyes now following a graceful stingray gliding overhead. "A lucky homebuyer might purchase a house at the right time, live in it for a few years, and then sell it for twice as much because of a massive upturn in the housing market. But these are the exceptions."

John raised an eyebrow. "And for most people?"

Matthew paused as they reached a large tank filled with vibrant coral and darting fish and continued, "For most people, home ownership doesn't work that way. The average person wants the investor's results, but they don't understand that the buying strategy is different."

John glanced at him with curiosity, "Different, how?"

"The typical investor buys a property and sells it for a profit," Matthew explained, turning to face John fully. "In this case, the motive and financial arrangement are fixed on making a profit from start to finish. The typical homebuyer, on the other hand, purchases a house as a dwelling place. It becomes a residence. The financial arrangement is different, and so is the outcome. Consequently, most average homeowners lose big money on their homes."

John frowned, his mind racing. "So you're saying homeownership is a financial trap?"

"In many cases, yes," Matthew replied, his tone somber. "Homeownership is the fifth cultural barrier to financial success. Unfortunately, how most of us buy houses in this country is one of the biggest hindrances to financial freedom."

John's face tightened with concern. "But aren't there benefits? I mean, I've always heard that owning a home is a good investment. I've bought a few houses myself, three, actually. I thought I was doing the right thing."

Matthew's gaze softened as he regarded John. "You did what most people do, John. You believed homeownership was a good investment because that's what you've been told. But were you sure, or did you believe you were doing the right thing based on what you've heard over the years?"

John was silent for a moment, his thoughts heavy. "I guess... I just believed it was the right thing to do. It's what everyone says, right? 'Why rent when you can buy?' 'Stop wasting your money by renting.'"

Matthew nodded, his expression sympathetic. "Exactly. Banks, mortgage companies, real estate agents, local governments—they've all been raving about the great value of homeownership for years. 'Buy a house, build equity, and get tax benefits.' It all sounds so promising. And yet, although nearly two-thirds of Americans own their homes, only some homeowners are financially better off than renters."

John's eyes narrowed in thought. "But why? If so many people own homes, shouldn't they be better off?"

"You would think so," Matthew said with a slight smile. "But the truth is, most homeowners are struggling to stay solvent because of cash flow issues. Meanwhile, the ones who stand to benefit the most from homeownership are the home builders, real estate agents, mortgage companies, the government, home retail outlets, and home repair companies."

John stared at the aquarium, the vibrant colors suddenly seeming less bright. "And the homeowner is left trying to maintain the property and keeping the taxes paid."

"Exactly," Matthew agreed. "According to the Federal National Mortgage Association, the top three reasons for buying a house are proximity to quality schools, safety, and financial incentives. But that financial incentive is often based on the assumption that a house is a good investment."

John shook his head slowly. "But if most people are financially unstable and know little about financial investments, how do they know that homebuying is an excellent choice?"

"That's the problem," Matthew replied. "Few people dive deep into real estate matters before buying a house. More often, they are led through the process from start to finish, without fully understanding what they're getting into."

John sighed, "I guess I've got a lot to think about."

Matthew placed a reassuring hand on John's shoulder. "We all do, John. If the reason for buying a house is personal, meaning convenience, safety, proximity to schools, or easy access to freeways, there's no argument then. The hope is that the motive behind the purchase justifies the cost."

John nodded, his brow furrowed in concentration. "But if someone is buying a house with the intention of financial gain, thinking it's a sure path to wealth, that's where the trouble starts, right?"

"Yes, you got that right," Matthew confirmed as they approached the dolphin show, the sound of water splashing and excited cheers growing louder. "When the intention is set on financial benefits—profit, gains, whatever—the reality is that homeownership can do the exact opposite, especially when purchased on a mortgage."

John frowned, watching the dolphins leap gracefully. "You mean it can actually deplete wealth instead of building it?"

"Yes," Matthew said, his tone firm. "A mortgage consumes your hard-earned income and restricts your ability to capitalize on other investments. It locks you into a financial commitment that can limit your freedom for decades."

They found seats near the back, where they could talk without disturbing others. As the show began, Matthew leaned in slightly, lowering his voice to ensure John could hear him over the noise.

"Remember," Matthew continued, "these conditions don't apply to homebuyers who purchase with cash. Buying a house with cash is a different story—it's a good idea. In fact, each year, millions of people take advantage of the opportunity. Did you know that in recent years, half of all homes sold in the US were bought with cash?"

John raised his eyebrows, clearly surprised. "Damn, are you serious?"

"Yes," Matthew agreed, watching as the dolphins performed a synchronized jump. "But the numbers soon dropped. Still, it's a practice that many prefer because of the unique advantages it provides."

"Like what?" John asked.

"Financial security, homeownership stability, financial leverage," Matthew listed, ticking them off on his fingers. "A cash purchase means no monthly payments, no interest, no debt. But even with a cash purchase, there are still a few minor issues to consider."

John shifted in his seat, turning his full attention to Matthew. "What kind of issues?"

"First, buying a home, whether with a mortgage or cash, is never entirely free from government control," Matthew explained. "If property taxes or liens aren't paid on time, the owner could potentially lose the property. And then there's the concern about putting too many liquid assets into one investment class. Some financial experts would advise against it because it minimizes diversification."

John nodded thoughtfully, absorbing the information. "So, you're saying that even with cash, it's not entirely risk-free, but it's still better than a mortgage?"

"Yes," Matthew confirmed. "I highly recommend a cash purchase instead of a mortgage purchase. My reasons will be apparent in a minute."

The show ended, and as the crowd began to disperse, Matthew and John remained seated, lost in their conversation.

"As I mentioned earlier," Matthew said, his tone more serious now, "purchasing a house on a mortgage is one of the biggest financial blunders in modern times. For most prospective homeowners, this will be their most significant debt obligation, and it will keep them trapped in a financial contract for years."

John frowned, "But isn't that just part of the process? I mean, most people don't see a problem with it."

"That's because most of us have been deceived," Matthew said, shaking his head. "Banks, mortgage companies, even the government—they all encourage the practice because they stand to gain from it. For them, it's a business transaction, not an emotional one."

"But for the homebuyer, it's personal," John added, his voice heavy with realization.

"Exactly," Matthew said, nodding. "The purchase is primarily emotional. We're trained to focus on the house's beauty, its location in the community, the potential for appreciation, and more. But could all of this be misleading? Is it possible that buying a house on credit is the most significant financial mistake we make?"

John leaned back in his seat, his mind racing. "How does that mistake play out in a typical home-buying scenario?"

Matthew leaned in closer, his voice taking on a more instructional tone as if guiding John through a mental exercise. "Let's say you're in the market to buy a house. You're married, with a combined gross income of $100,000 a year, or about $8,000 a month. You choose the right location and hire a real estate agent to help with the purchase."

John nodded, already picturing the scenario in his mind.

"But before you even start looking at houses, the agent decides to pre-qualify you to determine your range of purchase," Matthew continued. "This is standard in the industry—it saves time and hassle. The pre-qualification process determines your income stability, creditworthiness, and debt-to-income ratio."

"And based on that," John interjected, "you're told you can afford a sizeable mortgage."

"Exactly," Matthew confirmed. "In this case, you're qualified for up to $550,000, which gives you a lot of housing options. So, the agent takes you through various models, starting with the lower-priced homes, say around $250,000, then $350,000. But eventually, you fall in love with something that costs $550,000."

John sighed, already seeing where this was going. "And because you're pre-qualified, you think you can afford it."

"Right," Matthew said. "Unable to make a down payment, you finance the entire $550,000. Within 45-60 days, you move into your brand-new house. But before closing escrow, something catches your attention—your monthly mortgage payment will be around $3,577."

John winced at the number. "That's a lot."

"It is," Matthew agreed. "Most of that money will go toward interest payments. But by signing the documents, you're obligated to pay the debt and responsible for making those payments on time, rain or shine."

John rubbed his temples, the stress of the hypothetical situation weighing on him. "So, what are the financial facts of this purchase?"

Matthew didn't hesitate. "You borrowed $550,000 to buy the house. You have a 30-year, fixed-rate mortgage at 5 percent interest. Your monthly principal and interest payments are roughly $2,952. Add in $500 for property tax and $125 for mortgage insurance, and your monthly payment is approximately $3,577."

"And over 30 years..." John began, his voice trailing off.

"You'll pay $512,906 in interest alone," Matthew finished for him. "At the end of the 30 years, you will have paid your mortgage company $1,062,906—twice as much as the original mortgage."

John stared at him, wide-eyed. "That's... incredible."

"But it gets worse," Matthew continued, his tone unrelenting. "During those 30 years, you'll pay $180,000 in property taxes and $45,000 in mortgage insurance. When you add that to your principal and interest, your housing cost will be $1,287,906."

John let out a low whistle, his mind reeling. "That's more than double the cost of the house."

"And that's not even including upkeep," Matthew added. "Landscaping, painting, roof repairs, plumbing—

it all adds up. To break even, you'd have to sell the house for over $1,287,906."

John shook his head, overwhelmed by the numbers. "But can you even do that? Sell it for that much?"

"That depends on the condition of the house and the real estate market at the time of sale," Matthew said. "But before you even get to that point, you have more pressing matters. You're excited about your new home, making preparations to enjoy it, and you haven't realized the property is more than you can afford."

John slumped in his seat, "So, I should have gone for a less expensive house."

"Ideally, yes," Matthew agreed. "A $250,000 - $350,000 house would have been better for you. But this is common—most people purchase more houses than they can afford because the bigger house has everything they want. They become emotionally involved and ignore the high mortgage payments."

"And then there's the social aspect," John said, a bitter edge to his voice. "The bragging rights, the resale value..."

"Yes, exactly, John," Matthew said with a sigh. "People are driven by what sounds good, looks attractive, and feels right, not necessarily what makes financial sense. And because of that, they experience more financial problems down the road, but it's too soon to tell."

John looked down, his hands clenched into fists. "The ink is still wet on the documents."

"Yes," Matthew said gently. "And right now, you're too excited about the purchase to be rational. You now have the keys, and legally, the property is yours. But in the coming months, you'll spend additional money on the house—new furniture, a bigger TV, landscaping services. Most new homeowners spend $10,000 when they first move in, often on credit cards. You did the same thing, right?"

John nodded slowly, his eyes still on the sea creatures, but his mind now replaying the early days of his homeownership. He remembered the excitement, the thrill of decorating and swiping his credit card at every turn.

Matthew continued, "Legally, you're now a homeowner, but you're cash-poor. Everything—your house, the furniture, the appliances—was bought on credit. You haven't really thought about it because you were caught up in the excitement. But that's what I call the home-ownership illusion."

"I've gone through this," John admitted. "At first, it was all about the thrill—getting the keys, moving in, decorating. But now... it's like reality is catching up to me."

"In the months ahead," Matthew continued, "your financial reality will unfold in ways you hadn't anticipated. At first, everything seems great. You're living in your dream home, after all. But then you start struggling to make ends meet. Eight months in, the mortgage payment feels suffocating. It's eating up half of your combined net income, and suddenly, it's all you can think about."

John swallowed hard, his throat dry. "That's exactly it," he said, his voice barely above a whisper. "It's like the mortgage was this huge weight hanging over me. I was constantly thinking about it, worrying about making the payment."

Matthew's tone remained calm, but there was a firm edge to it. "After the mortgage, you've barely got enough to pay the minimums on your credit cards. You're worried, but you didn't realize that your mortgage pre-qualification was based on your gross income. Now, you're working with your net income, and it feels like the numbers don't add up. Even after cutting back on food, utilities, and recreation, you're barely scraping by."

John's face reddened with embarrassment. "I was cutting back on everything," he confessed. "I was barely going out anymore. I was trying to save on groceries, utilities—everything. But it was still not enough."

Matthew turned to him, his expression one of quiet concern. "The truth is, you were financially stifled, and you didn't even know how it happened. The stress was real, John. You were living in a beautiful home, driving nice cars, dressing well, but inside, you were struggling to stay afloat financially. The good thing was, nobody knew. But deep down, you knew—you were broke."

"I hate admitting it," John murmured. "I thought I was doing everything right, but... yeah, I was broke. And the worst part was, I didn't know how to fix it."

"This kind of situation," Matthew added, his voice gentle but unyielding, "is more common than you think. Millions of homeowners are in the same boat, struggling silently. We've learned to keep our money problems secret, but that doesn't make them any less real."

John let out a heavy sigh, the truth weighing on him. "I guess I just never thought it would happen to me," he said, almost to himself. "I thought I was smarter than that."

"For anyone in this situation, if things don't change soon," Matthew warned, "one must consider drastic measures. Working two jobs, selling the house, or even filing for bankruptcy again. You thought you were making financial headway, but the truth is, the house was another major hindrance to your financial success. It was constantly draining your income, reserves, and credit to function. And some people borrow against the equity in their home to start a business, that becomes another debt—a second mortgage that needs to be repaid."

John's mind raced, the implications of Matthew's words crashing down on him like a tidal wave. "Well, I couldn't imagine selling the house," he said, his voice tinged with panic. "It was *my* home, the place I worked so hard to build. But I had to sell it anyways."

Matthew placed a hand on John's shoulder, "The house you bought was way out of your financial league. A $250,000 to $300,000 home would have been ideal. But in your excitement, you underestimated the demands of the mortgage, the hidden costs of homeownership, and the ongoing needs of your family. You overextended yourself to the point of financial hemorrhaging."

John nodded slowly, "I just... I didn't think it through. I was so focused on the dream that I didn't stop to consider the reality."

"Some financial knowledge and foresight could have prevented these problems," Matthew concluded. "In the next session, we'll discuss with detail the financial realities of homeownership—things that were deliberately left out earlier for the sake of brevity. But know this, John: this home-ownership scenario isn't just your story. It's the story of millions of Americans who overextend themselves financially, often to impress others, and end up struggling to keep everything together."

John felt exhaustion fill him, the full weight of his financial missteps pressing down on him. But beneath the fatigue, there was hope. "I don't want to be stuck in this cycle," he said quietly, meeting Matthew's gaze. "I want to fix this. I want to learn how to get out of this mess."

"The best advice I can give you about homeownership," Matthew began reflectively, "comes from my own experience."

John shifted his attention from the glowing jellyfish floating by to Matthew, sensing that what he was about to hear was more than just advice—it was a hard-learned lesson.

"In my thirties," Matthew continued, "I bought my first home. It was an exciting time—I had a young family, and I wanted a place where we could grow, where we could build memories. Later, as we got more comfortable, I upgraded to a second home and then a third. Each time, I thought I was making a smart move—improving our living situation and investing in our future. But looking back, those thirty years of homeownership kept me broke, though they did make me wiser."

John frowned, surprised. "You kept upgrading, and you were still broke? And I thought owning more property was supposed to mean more security, more wealth."

Matthew shook his head with a wry smile. "That's the illusion. Here are five things I didn't know about homeownership—things I wish someone had told me back then."

They paused in front of a massive tank where a whale swam gracefully. Its fluid movements seemed opposite to the tension John felt growing in his chest.

"First," Matthew said, holding up a finger, "if you must buy a house, don't approach it as a financial investment. Real estate can deplete your wealth-building capacity over time. You're always putting money into the property—mortgage, maintenance, taxes, insurance—most of which ends up on credit cards, compromising your financial position."

John crossed his arms, his brows furrowed in thought. "But isn't real estate supposed to be one of the safest investments? Everyone says buying a home is better than renting because it builds equity."

Matthew nodded slowly. "That's what I thought too. But the reality is different. A house isn't a traditional investment. It's a liability that constantly drains your resources. Even if it appreciates in value, the costs associated with maintaining it often outweigh the gains."

He turned to John, his eyes serious. "Second, don't put additional cash into the property if you're buying it on a mortgage. It's a mistake I made too many times. Your savings are real cash—money that belongs to you. But once you pour it into a house, especially when you're still paying a mortgage, that money goes away forever. It ends up with the lienholder, not in your pocket."

John exhaled sharply. "I guess I never really thought about it that way. I always figured that the more I put in, the more I'd get out when I sold the house."

"It's a common misconception," Matthew said, placing a hand on John's shoulder. "But the truth is, the money you put in is often swallowed by the costs of owning and maintaining the home. And the market is volatile; you can't always rely on it to recover your investment."

As they moved further along the exhibit, the vibrant colors of tropical fish danced around them, but John's mind was now focused entirely on Matthew's words.

"Third," Matthew continued, his tone becoming more insistent, "don't let others, or the culture, pressure you into buying a house before you're financially ready. The real estate industry thrives on deception—banks, mortgage companies, even the government—they all sell this idea of the "American Dream". But saddling yourself with the biggest debt of your life isn't help; it's a trap."

John looked away, the truth of Matthew's words hitting him harder than he expected. "I see what you mean," he said quietly. "When I bought our place, everyone told me it was the best decision I could make— that I was investing in our future. But then…it just felt like I was tied down."

Matthew's expression softened. "It's a common story, John. Once you're a homeowner, you're liable for everything—the mortgage, the upkeep, the taxes. And that liability can become a massive burden."

They paused near a tank where a lone sea turtle glided through the water.

"Fourth," Matthew said, "don't count on your home's equity as part of your assets. The money in home equity doesn't belong to you. If you tap into it, it becomes a loan—a debt you must repay. And that equity depends on the market, which, as we've seen, can be unpredictable. If you sell the house to get the cash, you're suddenly homeless unless you rent or buy another property."

John let out a slow breath, processing the implications. "So even the equity isn't really mine until I sell the house?"

"Exactly," Matthew confirmed. "And even then, it's not free money—it's just the return of what you've already spent, and often it doesn't even cover what you put into the property."

They continued walking; the soft hum of the aquarium's filters added a background to the conversation.

"And fifth," Matthew said, turning to John, "continue renting for as long as possible. The mortgage and real estate industries often paint renters as fools, throwing money away each month. But the truth is, nothing consumes more of a person's income than homeownership. Renters generally spend less on housing because they avoid all the hidden costs that come with owning a home."

John looked skeptical. "But what about the equity? Isn't it better to put that money into something you own rather than rent?"

Matthew gave a small, sad smile. "That's the pitch, isn't it? But let me ask you this—how much of your mortgage payment goes towards interest? In the first year, it's about 85%, and after five years, it's still around the same number. That means during those years, only a tiny fraction of what you pay actually reduces your principal. The rest goes to the bank."

John's eyes widened as the numbers sank in. "I had no idea it was that high..."

"And don't forget," Matthew continued, "the other costs—property taxes, home insurance, upkeep, remodeling, even flood insurance. All those things add up to tens of thousands of dollars that you'll never get back. As a renter, once you pay the rent, you're done. The landlord handles everything else."

John rubbed his face, "So, you're saying I should have kept renting? And now... what? Sell the house? Go back to renting?"

Matthew's voice softened, full of understanding. "What's done is done, John. I'm not saying you should take drastic steps right now. But with your current experience and this knowledge, you'll be in a better position to consider your housing options in the future. Maybe renting is the better choice for you in the long run. For now, though, focus on stabilizing your finances, and keep this information in mind."

John nodded, "I never thought about it like this... I wish I had known all this before."

Matthew smiled gently. "We all wish we'd known these things earlier, John. But the important thing is that you're learning now. When you're ready to make your next move—whether it's buying another home or sticking with renting—you'll do it with your eyes wide open."

As they left the aquarium, stepping out into the bright sunlight, John felt somewhat relieved and hopeful. Now, he had a clearer understanding of what he had to do.

CHAPTER 15

◇∞◇

A Baby or Money?

Matthew and John arrived at the HBK Tours shop in La Jolla just as the sun began to rise over the Pacific. The salty air was cool and refreshing, with the faint sound of waves crashing against the cliffs nearby. The shop itself was modest, tucked between a surf shack and a café. Its wooden exterior was painted a light blue, with a sign reading "HBK Tours" in bright yellow letters. A row of bikes, gleaming in the morning light, was lined up out front, ready for the day's adventure.

Matthew led John inside, where the shop smelled of fresh leather and metal polish. A cheerful guide wearing the HBK Tours logo on his shirt greeted them with a smile. "Welcome to HBK Tours! You two ready for a ride today?" he asked.

"Yes, we're excited to explore La Jolla," Matthew replied.

The guide nodded and directed them to a rack of helmets, gesturing for them to pick out their sizes. Matthew chose a sleek black helmet, while John picked one in bright blue. The guide then walked them over to the bikes. They were top-of-the-line, with lightweight frames and sturdy tires designed for navigating both the paved paths and the occasional rough terrain.

"Here you go," the guide said, handing them each a bike. "These are fully tuned up and ready to go. The trails around here are beautiful, especially in the early morning. You'll have some great views of the coastline."

Matthew and John strapped on their helmets and adjusted the straps under their chins. They checked the fit of their bikes, adjusting the seats and testing the brakes. Satisfied, Matthew turned to John, a thoughtful expression on his face.

"John," Matthew began as they mounted their bikes, "Certain things happen to us naturally as we go through life. One of them is having children, often shortly after marriage. Otherwise, the circumstances through which children are born into this world vary from family to family."

They began to pedal, their bikes moving smoothly over the pavement as they headed towards the scenic coastal paths. The morning light reflected off the ocean, casting a golden glow on the water. John listened intently as Matthew continued.

"As you know," Matthew said, "children are a significant part of almost every household worldwide. This is because most people believe having kids is lovely. They complete the family. They bring joy that can't be found anywhere else."

John nodded, focusing on the path ahead. "That's true."

Matthew glanced over at John. "But these days, not everyone feels the same way about children," he said. "The main reason is the cost of raising them. Having and raising children is what I consider the sixth cultural barrier to financial success."

Matthew and John rode their bikes side by side along the winding coastal path. The sound of the waves crashing against the cliffs below provided a soothing backdrop to their conversation. The air smelled of salt, and the occasional cry of a seagull swooped overhead. As they reached a scenic lookout point, they slowed their pace, taking in the panoramic view of the ocean stretching out to the horizon.

Matthew turned to John, "John, your children are in high school now and possibly getting ready for college. Over the years, you've spent a significant amount of money raising them, including child support. And, like most people, you may not have fully considered the costs."

John nodded, "Yeah, I guess I never really added it all up. I just thought of it as part of being a parent."

Matthew adjusted his grip on the handlebars, glancing out at the ocean. "Few people take the time to compute these expenses," he said. "Others ignore the costs because they feel obligated to spend the money. But the reality is that the expense of raising children is immense. This financial burden falls directly on the people who bring them into the world. Often, that cost makes the difference between financial independence and simply getting by."

John was quiet for a moment, digesting Matthew's words. He looked down at the ground, his brow furrowed in thought. "I get what you're saying. It's a huge responsibility, but isn't that just part of life?"

Matthew nodded. "It is, but we need to be aware of the impact it has on our financial goals. Despite the financial challenges associated with child-rearing, some people are determined to have kids. This desire is often referred to as 'baby fever.' It's a bona fide emotion that varies in intensity in both men and women, usually developing between ages 18 and 45. You know how it is—women at that age can get pregnant anytime, though it can also happen before age 18 or after age 45."

John smiled slightly. "Yeah, I've seen it happen. Friends from high school having kids before we even graduated."

Matthew continued, "Most couples want to be well-prepared before seriously considering having children. That usually means getting college out of the way, settling into a stable career, having a good amount of money saved, and living in a reasonably safe neighborhood. But these things are not always expected or planned. This is especially true for pregnancy and childbirth. Young couples are often ill-prepared when a pregnancy occurs. Many are in low-paying jobs or dealing with college assignments when they get the news."

John looked thoughtful. "Yes, It's tough. Most people are juggling so much—trying to pay off debt, advance in their careers, and then a child comes along."

"Exactly," Matthew said, picking up speed as they rode downhill. "People between the ages of 25 and 45 are often carrying the most debt—large mortgages, car payments, high credit card balances. Statistically, this is also the time when they're working hard to advance in their careers, aiming to maximize income, achieve a specific lifestyle, or at least maintain their current one. Adding children to these converging events is financially risky for any family except those with the financial resources to sustain the responsibility."

They rode in silence for a moment, the breeze tugging at their clothes. Then Matthew spoke again, "Despite the financial burden, many young couples want children as early as possible, even if they don't have a solid reason beyond the natural inclination to procreate. Some feel a sense of fulfilling a cosmic responsibility, while others are just curious to see what their children would look like."

John chuckled. "I guess that makes sense. Everyone wants to see a little version of themselves running around."

Matthew smiled, but his tone remained serious. "Yes, but after the first child, a woman's perspective often changes. The so-called 'baby fever' drops drastically. The pain of childbirth, the responsibility of caring for the first child, and the challenges of raising them combine to make a profound statement. It's a lot to handle."

John glanced at Matthew. "And what about those who decide they don't want kids at all?"

"Good question," Matthew replied. "Some women don't want children and will most likely never change their minds. They're often referred to as 'childfree' or 'childless by choice.' Currently, one in five American women wants nothing to do with pregnancy, childbirth, and the responsibility of raising children. This number is growing rapidly. For these women, having children means less time, money, and freedom. They're usually more educated, work in professional careers, live in urban areas and are less likely to be associated with religious groups. For them, not having children isn't just a choice; it's part of their identity."

John nodded. "I've met a few people like that. They seem really sure about their decision."

Matthew shifted on his bike seat, considering his words. "Looking at both sides of the issue, it's not about who is right or wrong. Both sides have valid arguments. The best approach is to remain neutral and recognize that having or not having children is a deeply personal decision. It should be treated with respect and consideration."

John's expression softened as he listened. "So, the goal here is to understand the costs and implications?"

"Exactly," Matthew agreed. "Our focus is to highlight the financial costs associated with raising children. As you'll see, this is a responsibility fewer people should undertake without careful thought. Considering all the factors affecting people's finances, there's no guarantee that being childless will lead to financial success. Even with a significant income, poor financial decisions can keep someone broke throughout life."

They reached another lookout point, pausing to catch their breath and admire the view. Matthew continued, "People tend to spend money on activities that align with their interests. And sometimes, these financial decisions don't make sense—whether it's overspending on material things or, in some cases, choosing to have children when already struggling financially."

John sighed, looking out at the ocean. "It's all about making informed choices, isn't it?"

Matthew nodded. "Yes. For families already struggling with debt and financial obligations, adding a child can worsen their situation. According to the U.S. Department of Agriculture, parents with an annual income of sixty-four grand or more will spend about ninety-eight grand raising a child by their sixth birthday—that's about sixteen grand a year. Daycare alone can cost between $300 to $1,500 a month, with the average being $972. For someone making $12.50 an hour, that's about half their monthly wage."

John looked surprised. "That's a lot of money."

"And it's just the beginning," Matthew said. "Those first six years are only a fraction of the total cost. Raising a child until age eighteen can cost an additional $192,000. So, in total, parents could spend around $290,000, not including college. College adds another substantial amount—about $160,000 for a four-year private college. The total can approach $450,000 by the time the child graduates. Almost half a million dollars to raise one child from birth through college."

John shook his head. "No wonder some people are hesitant to have kids. That's a massive financial commitment."

Matthew agreed. "Absolutely. Cost is one of the biggest reasons why some people choose not to have children. They value their personal freedom and flexibility, which the child-free option provides. Others choose to wait until they're financially stable before starting a family. Finding the right balance can be challenging. Some limit themselves to one or two children. I was one of those who decided to have no more than two. But even then, I couldn't afford to send them to college without loans. Later, I helped them repay their student loans as I became more wealthy. They're determined to succeed, and I support them fully."

John looked thoughtful. "It sounds like planning and understanding your financial limits is really important."

Matthew nodded. "It is. Some people struggle to draw a line between having and not having children. They let emotions drive their decisions. They believe love and family will somehow provide for their children, ignoring the harsh reality that millions live in extreme poverty. When parents live in poverty, their children suffer the most."

He took a deep breath, then continued, "The point isn't to discourage young couples from having children but to make them aware of the financial implications. Limiting the number of children might be wise for those aiming for financial success. The more children people have, the more they'll spend on them, leaving fewer resources to achieve their goals. But ultimately, the choice is personal. Couples can have as many children as they want, and having children doesn't automatically mean a life of poverty. Some individuals use their family as motivation to strive for financial prosperity."

John smiled. "That's a positive way to look at it."

Matthew returned the smile. "Yes, but it's important to recognize that for most, the pursuit of wealth often takes a backseat to the immediate needs of their family. Whether one decides to have children, pursue financial success, or do both, awareness of the costs involved is essential. The important thing is to make informed decisions that align with personal values and financial goals."

As they resumed their ride, the conversation lingered like the ocean breeze. John yelled through the breeze loud enough for Matthew to hear. "So what do you recommend?" John asked, "It seems like no matter what decision you make, there are serious trade-offs."

Matthew nodded and slowed his pace, "It's not an easy question to answer, John. I think the best approach is to make decisions based on where you live and your current circumstances. First and foremost, you have to decide if having children is right for you. For some, the answer might be no, and that's okay. For others, it might be yes, but with a clear understanding of the financial and emotional commitments involved." Matthew paused, letting the burden of his words sink in.

"In some countries," he continued, "like China, there are government-imposed limits on the number of children a family can have. These policies are controversial, but they are rooted in concerns about overpopulation and the strain on national resources. While some may disagree with this kind of control, from an economic perspective, it does make sense. It's a way to ensure that every family can provide for their children without overwhelming the country's infrastructure and resources."

John tilted his head, mulling over Matthew's point. "So, you're saying that population control measures like that can actually benefit society?"

"Yes," Matthew replied, leaning forward slightly. "At least from a resource management standpoint. It's about protecting the long-term sustainability of a country's population. But, of course, in places like the United States, we don't have those restrictions. Here, the number of children a family decides to have is entirely up to them, which can lead to a different set of challenges."

John interjected, "Like the issues you mentioned before, with child poverty rates and families struggling to make ends meet."

"Exactly," Matthew agreed. "When people ignore the costs of raising children in favor of what they desire emotionally, the number of children can exceed what the family can reasonably support. In the US, more than 16 million children are living in poverty, which is about a quarter of the child population. Families with incomes under about twenty thousand for a household of four face immense difficulties. Those children often experience starvation, lack of proper healthcare, and inadequate education, which perpetuates the cycle of poverty."

John's expression turned more serious. "It sounds like you're suggesting that people think about having children more rationally. But isn't there more to it than just economics?"

Matthew smiled gently. "Of course, there is. Family planning is deeply personal and involves many emotional and cultural factors. But if your goal is to achieve financial stability and provide a good life for your children, you need to think about the economic implications. Having too many children can stretch your resources thin, making it difficult to save for emergencies, invest in your future, or even provide the basic necessities. You want to ensure your children grow up in a safe environment where they can thrive, not one where they're struggling to survive."

John nodded, a contemplative look on his face. "It makes sense when you put it that way. But how do you balance the desire to have a family with the need to be financially responsible?"

Matthew shrugged slightly. "There's no one-size-fits-all answer, but it starts with planning and being honest about what you can afford. Ask yourself what kind of life you want your children to have. Do you want them to be safe, happy, and have access to opportunities? Or do you want them to struggle with poverty and uncertainty? By considering these questions before you have children, you can make more informed decisions that align with your financial goals and personal values."

He continued, "This isn't about denying the desire to have children or saying that people should only have kids if they're wealthy. It's about incorporating sensibility in family planning. People shouldn't let emotions drive their decisions to have children without considering the consequences. The world doesn't need more children who are neglected or starved because their parents were unprepared. And when that happens, the burden often falls on the community and society."

John took a deep breath, feeling a bit more grounded. "You're right. This is a big decision that needs to be approached with a level head."

Matthew smiled warmly. "Exactly, John. You have the power to shape your financial future in a way that will be more gratifying, both for you and your family. By planning carefully, you can achieve a balance that allows you to enjoy the experience of raising children while also working towards your personal and financial goals. It's all about making thoughtful choices and not losing sight of what's truly important."

While John was pondering, Matthew checked his watch, noting the time. "Looks like it's about time we head back," he said, glancing over at John. The afternoon sun had begun its slow descent, casting a golden glow over La Jolla's rocky coastline. They had spent the past few hours riding along the winding bike paths, the Pacific Ocean's rhythmic waves crashing nearby, invigorating them.

"Yeah, I guess so," John replied. He had enjoyed the ride and their talk, finding it both enlightening and thought-provoking. "Time flies when you're having a good discussion," he added with a small smile.

Matthew nodded in agreement, steering his bike towards the shop. "It's true. Conversations like this are important. They make you think about what really matters, you know?"

As they pedaled back toward HBK Tours, the shop where they had rented their bikes and helmets, John let his thoughts wander over everything they had discussed. Matthew's words had given him a lot to consider. The quiet streets of La Jolla, lined with lush greenery and upscale homes, seemed to mirror the tranquility he felt after their conversation.

They soon arrived at the bike rental shop. The shop's blue-and-white awning fluttered in the breeze. Matthew hopped off his bike first, walking it over to the rack outside the shop. He lifted his helmet off, running a hand through his hair, before hanging the helmet on the handlebars.

John followed suit, unbuckling his helmet and handing it over to the shop attendant who was waiting for them. The attendant, a young man with sun-bleached hair and a perpetual tan, greeted them with a friendly smile. "How was the ride?" he asked, taking the bikes from them.

"It was great," Matthew replied, stretching his arms. "Perfect weather for it, and the views were spectacular as always."

"Glad to hear it," the attendant said, wheeling the bikes back inside the shop.

Matthew turned to John, extending his hand. "Thanks for coming out today. I hope our conversation gave you some things to think about."

John shook his hand firmly. "It did, Matthew. More than you know. I appreciate you taking the time to talk through these things. It's not something people often discuss openly."

Matthew smiled. "That's why it's important to have these conversations. To make sure we're making informed decisions and not just going with the flow. We all have to take responsibility for the choices we make, especially when it comes to something as significant as family planning and financial stability."

They both stood there for a moment, the bustling sounds of the late afternoon surrounding them—people chatting at the café, the distant crash of waves, the occasional honk of a car horn.

"So, same time next week?" John asked.

"Absolutely," Matthew replied with a nod.

John smiled, feeling a surge of optimism. "I'll see you next week, then."

With that, they parted ways. John watched as Matthew walked down the street, his figure blending into the crowd. He turned and began his own walk back to his car, his mind buzzing with thoughts of the future, finances, and the kind of life he wanted to build.

CHAPTER 16

❦

A Second Look at the Joneses

As they paddled through the calm waters of the La Jolla coastline, the sun sparkled off the gentle waves. The cliffs loomed above them, a towering reminder of nature's ancient artistry. John couldn't help but glance around in awe, his kayak gliding smoothly with Matthew leading the way. The sound of the ocean lapping against the sandstone echoed in the natural chamber, creating an almost melodic hum.

"These caves are incredible," John said, his voice carrying over the soft roar of the waves. "I had no idea they were this old."

Matthew gave a slight nod, his paddle cutting through the water with practiced ease. "Yeah, the sea's been at work on these cliffs for millions of years. It's a reminder of how time shapes everything—slow and steady."

As they entered the shadow of the first sea cave, the temperature dropped slightly, and the air became thick with the smell of salt and damp rock. The soft slosh of their paddles reverberated off the narrow walls, creating an almost meditative atmosphere.

After a moment, Matthew broke the silence. "The thing is, people think they've got all the time in the world to build wealth. But most of them spend it chasing after things that aren't even their own goals. It's like paddling against the current, constantly trying to match everyone else's pace."

John looked over, intrigued. "You mean, like competing with your neighbors?"

Matthew nodded, a small smile playing at the corners of his mouth. "Exactly. You've heard the phrase 'Keeping up with the Joneses,' right?"

John chuckled. "Yeah, that one's been around forever."

Matthew's face grew more serious. "It's not just a saying, though. It's the seventh cultural barrier to financial success. People look around at what others have—bigger houses, newer cars, fancy vacations—and they start thinking they need the same or better. The problem is, they're measuring their worth by someone else's standards."

John tilted his head thoughtfully, the gentle rocking of the kayak keeping him in rhythm with Matthew's words. "I guess I've been guilty of that, too. But it's hard not to when society is constantly throwing these images in your face."

"That's exactly the trap," Matthew said, his voice steady but firm. "The comparison becomes a competition, and the competition becomes a cycle. You end up spending money on things that don't actually bring value to your life—just to keep pace. You drown in debt, trying to match an illusion."

They drifted into another cave, its entrance dark and mysterious. Rays of sunlight pierced through small openings in the sandstone, illuminating the intricate textures of the cave walls.

"Look at these cliffs," Matthew said, his eyes scanning the ancient rock formations. "They've been here, unchanged, while the world outside shifts. That's how our financial foundation should be. Solid, consistent. Not based on what the world says you should have, but what you truly need and value."

John absorbed the words while his gaze followed Matthew's, admiring the timeless beauty around them. As they reached the Clam Cave, a broad chamber with walls that seemed to ripple like waves carved from stone, Matthew pointed to the natural patterns etched into the sandstone. "You see how the ocean carves its way through the rock over centuries, creating these intricate designs?" he asked. "It's slow, methodical, with purpose. That's how we should be with our own lives—clear, deliberate. But instead, most people rush to fill the void with things they don't need, just like these caves, cluttered and filled over time."

John nodded, gazing at the smooth walls and the light filtering in through the cave's entrance. The air here was cooler, more still, as if even nature knew to take its time.

Matthew continued, his voice echoing slightly. "The practice of imitating others is widespread but dangerous. Psychologically, when people mimic the lifestyles of others, they start to lose sight of their own potential. They stop growing, stop achieving, and gradually become less of themselves. They forget what they truly value and chase after what others say is important."

John's paddle rested across his knees as he considered Matthew's words. "Yeah, I see that happening a lot. People going into debt just to have the latest gadgets or bigger houses, but at what cost?"

"Exactly," Matthew said. "Financially, it's devastating. Sure, a few people can afford to buy the things they want, but millions more stretch beyond their means. They're driven by the need to keep up, to display their wealth even when it's not real. And the result is what you see in most homes—excessiveness."

John glanced at Matthew, curious. "Excessiveness?"

Matthew leaned back slightly in his kayak, resting his arms. "Yeah. It's not just about spending money. The accumulation of stuff leads to waste, clutter, and eventually hoarding. It's a vicious cycle—people buy things they don't need, fill their homes with possessions, and then struggle to maintain control over their own space. It drains resources, both financial and emotional."

The waves lapped gently against the walls of the cave, and for a moment, they sat in silence, listening to the rhythmic sound. It was peaceful here, but John could sense Matthew's words pressing in on him.

"I'm sure you've seen it," Matthew added, his tone lighter now as if inviting John to reflect. "Look around any neighborhood—people's garages packed to the ceiling with stuff. Heck, maybe even your own home."

John frowned, thinking back to his childhood home. "Yeah, now that you mention it... there's a lot of stuff. People have boxes in the attic they haven't touched in years. And I've seen garages so full, you can barely walk through them, let alone park a car."

Matthew nodded. "That's the thing—almost every home in America has more material possessions than needed. It's like we've convinced ourselves that having more makes us more. But all that stuff just ends up collecting dust, cluttering our lives, and sometimes leading to something far worse: hoarding."

"Hoarding?" John asked, raising an eyebrow. "You mean like those extreme cases you see on TV?"

Matthew shifted in his seat, his voice calm but serious. "Hoarding starts small. It's a compulsive need to collect and keep things, even when they no longer serve a purpose. People tell themselves they might need it someday, but that day rarely comes. And as the clutter grows, it takes over—physically, emotionally, and mentally. Spaces meant for living become storage rooms, and that can lead to bigger problems—like poor ventilation, fire hazards, pests, and even family conflicts."

John's face tightened with concern. "I never really thought about it that way. I mean, I've seen clutter, but I never connected it to something so harmful."

"Most people don't," Matthew replied. "Some think it's just a quirk or a phase, but it's deeper than that. People with hoarding tendencies don't always realize they have a problem, and that's part of what makes it so dangerous. It's not just an inconvenience; it can create serious health risks and even economic hardships. Families argue over it—some don't mind the clutter, but others can't stand it."

They paddled farther into the cave, the light dimming as the entrance grew smaller in the distance. John's thoughts seemed to darken with the cave, the weight of the conversation sinking in. "So, is hoarding really connected to 'Keeping up with the Joneses'?"

"Absolutely," Matthew said. "It's all about the need to feel like we're enough, that we measure up. People believe their worth is tied to their possessions, so they buy more, even when they don't need or can't afford it. The more they have, the better they think they'll feel about themselves. But it's a hollow feeling, and soon after the purchase, those things get shoved into closets or garages, forgotten. And that's where the stockpiling begins."

John let out a long breath, thinking about his own habits. "I guess I'm guilty of that too, holding onto stuff that I might never use."

Matthew gave him a sympathetic look. "You're not alone. It's a mindset most of us have. But once you realize the trap, you can start making changes. It's not about never buying anything again; it's about being intentional. Figure out what really adds value to your life and let go of the rest."

The kayak glided effortlessly through the narrow passage between two towering cliffs. John's paddle sliced through the water as he absorbed everything Matthew had been saying.

Matthew, keeping his pace steady, glanced over at John. "You know, buying things in moderation isn't always a bad thing. A lot of people can make purchases without going overboard. But the real issue is when we can't part with what we collect."

John looked over, catching a faint ripple of reflection on the dark water. "Yeah, I've seen it. People buy something they think they need, and even if they never use it, they hang onto it. It's like… some kind of guilt."

"Exactly," Matthew said. "There's guilt attached to those purchases. It's as if getting rid of the item means admitting it wasn't needed in the first place. So, we keep moving those things from house to house, telling ourselves they'll be useful someday."

They paddled deeper into the cave, where the walls narrowed. Matthew's voice echoed, "Meanwhile, we keep buying more, stacking onto the pile until we run out of space. Closets fill up, so we use the attic. When that's full, we overflow into the garage. It's a cycle that people fall into without realizing it."

John nodded, grimacing at the truth of it. He thought of his old home, his garage cluttered with items he rarely touched. "I can see it happening. It's easy to ignore how much money goes into it, too."

"That's what makes keeping up with the Joneses so dangerous," Matthew said, his tone calm but pointed. "The economy of wealthy nations thrives on it. People see things—new gadgets, fashionable clothes, the latest tech—and they buy without thinking. It's impulsive. They see someone else with it and feel like they need it, too."

John sighed, his paddle briefly stilled. "And it's everywhere. Advertising, social media—it all pushes us to want more."

Matthew gave a firm nod. "Right. It's no accident. In affluent countries like the US, nonessential spending has grown faster than essential spending. Jewelry, dining out, toys—these are the things that are slowly eating away at people's finances. Spending on nonessential items is increasing faster than on essentials."

They reached an open cavern, where the ceiling opened up slightly to allow a stream of light to pour down. The water sparkled beneath them, but Matthew's words remained heavy.

"The Bureau of Economic Analysis shows that a significant portion of the average household income is spent on things people don't actually need," Matthew explained, his paddle gliding smoothly through the water. "It makes no difference how much money people make; a big chunk of it always goes toward nonessential purchases."

John's brow furrowed, the reality of those numbers sinking in. "I believe you."

"Across the country, this unnecessary spending adds up to trillions of dollars every year," Matthew continued. "Think about that. Two trillion dollars that could be going into savings, investments, or toward building wealth, but instead, it's sitting in our closets and garages."

John was silent, processing the enormity of it all. He looked around at the beauty of the cave—the ancient stone that had been shaped by time and patience. "It's like we're burying our futures under piles of stuff," he said softly.

Matthew gave him a knowing look. "Exactly. On the surface, much of your income spent on nonessentials might not seem like a big deal. But when you add that to an already strained budget, with living expenses, debt, taxes, and other obligations, it's no wonder so many people feel stuck."

They drifted in silence for a moment, the only sound the quiet lapping of water against the kayak. Matthew's voice was gentle but firm when he spoke again. "It takes money to make money. And when so much of it is misdirected toward things that don't matter, you lose time, opportunity, and wealth. People wonder why they can't get ahead, but the truth is right in front of them. Keeping up with the Joneses is slowly draining their financial resources."

John let out a frustrated breath. "It's like chasing a mirage. You think having more will make you happier or more successful, but all it does is weigh you down."

Matthew smiled at his friend's realization. "That's exactly it. The practice is fashionable, sure, but in the end, it's financially debilitating. People reach beyond their means to buy things they can't afford, and the money that could have been used to build wealth is spent on trivial things. It's a tragic cycle."

John glanced down at the water, his reflection distorted by the ripples. "I guess I never realized how much harm I was doing to myself by holding onto that mindset."

Matthew's eyes softened. "A lot of people don't see it until it's too late. Years pass, and they look back, wondering what went wrong. The key is recognizing the pattern now and finding ways to stop it. Learn to control the urge to spend on things that don't really matter."

As they exited the cave and paddled back into the bright sunlight, John's face showed a newfound determination. "I'm ready to make some changes," he said. "I've been wasting too much time and money on things that don't matter."

As they paddled deeper into the cool, echoing chambers of the sea cave, Matthew's voice carried with the rhythmic splashing of water against the kayak. "The whole concept of 'Keeping up with the Joneses' is at the heart of why so many people spend without thinking. Most of us make purchases because they make us feel a certain way or they help us fit in. There's a sense of belonging when you own something that's popular or fashionable. You feel connected to others, and that's a powerful thing. But here's the catch—while the instant gratification feels good, it's chipping away at your future. Every impulsive buy takes away from the cash you need to build something meaningful in life."

John dipped his paddle into the water, reflecting. "It's easy to forget about that when you're caught up in the moment."

Matthew nodded knowingly. "That's the problem. So, if you have an impulse buying habit, it's crucial to recognize it. Start by becoming aware of that sudden urge to buy something—whether it's something to eat, wear, or drive. Ask yourself: do I really need this? What is it adding to my life? The more conscious you are of these decisions, the easier it becomes to change them. Instead of spending, make it a habit to ask, 'How can this money better my financial situation?' It might mean choosing to save instead of splurging. And let me tell you, when you start to see those savings grow, you'll feel that same satisfaction, but it will be lasting."

John smirked, half-joking, "So, no more upgrading my phone every year?"

"Yes, exactly," Matthew chuckled. "Keep using that phone until it's genuinely broken or too outdated to function properly. The desire for the latest gadgets is one of the easiest traps to fall into. And advertisements don't help, do they? With phrases like 'You deserve it' or 'You're worth it,' they prey on your emotions, making you feel like buying something will improve your self-worth."

John's expression turned thoughtful. "It's true. I never realized how much those ads get to me."

"Most of us don't," Matthew said, his paddle slicing through the water as they moved forward. "If you find yourself feeling like you need to buy something to feel better, maybe it's time to talk to someone about it. Emotional spending can be a sign of something deeper, but addressing it will do wonders for both your mental and financial health."

They approached the entrance of another cave, the light filtering through the opening casting shimmering reflections on the water's surface. "Then there are other simple ways to cut back," Matthew continued. "Start with things like cooking more at home instead of eating out all the time. Skip the snacks, and not only will you save money, but you'll be healthier too. And for goodness' sake, avoid buying things just because they're on sale. Just because something is cheaper doesn't mean it's free. You're still spending money that could be saved."

John grimaced, recalling the times he'd bought things on a whim just because of a discount. "I've definitely fallen for that one. It adds up, doesn't it?"

"It does," Matthew confirmed. "And if you're using a credit card to make those purchases, you're paying even more in the long run because of interest. The item might have been on sale, but you end up paying more than it's worth over time. This is especially true when it comes to unnecessary luxuries, like concert or sports tickets. Sure, the memories might be fun for a moment, but if you're sacrificing your financial future for those short-lived experiences, you have to ask yourself what's more important."

As the kayak drifted into a calmer section of the cave, John looked around, taking in the natural beauty. "It's strange how much I haven't thought about any of this before. It's like I've just been following along without question."

"That's because most people don't think about it," Matthew said. "We get swept up in cultural influences—advertisements, traditions, peer pressure, even the perception of how we should live. But we have the power to make our own financial decisions. You have to learn to ignore those external pressures and decide what's right for your family and for your future. The next time you're tempted to buy something just because it looks good or everyone else has it, remember that the real winner is the one who keeps their money, not the one who spends it."

John let out a long breath, nodding. "I see that now."

Matthew smiled. "Good. The key is setting boundaries for yourself. Eliminate as many unnecessary expenses as possible and save that money. You'll feel a real sense of accomplishment. It's about being smart and intentional with how you spend. Practice doing what's best for you and your family, not what society tells you."

They floated in silence for a few moments, the sound of the ocean filling the space. "In the end," Matthew concluded, "when you buy something, your cash is gone forever. But if you hold onto it, you're the one who wins. Let that be you."

John met his gaze, "I'm going to start working on that."

Matthew gave him a nod of approval, "Good. Remember, it's a journey, not an overnight change. But each step you take will make a difference."

They paddled in silence for a while, the rhythmic swish of the oars cutting through the water and the soft sound of the waves against the sandstone walls of the cave system echoing around them. The bright sunlight outside filtered through the entrance of the cave, and as they paddled toward the open water, the contrast between the shadows of the cave and the bright sunlit sea seemed symbolic of the mental clarity John was starting to experience.

The kayak tour had ended as the two men glided smoothly back to the sandy shore of La Jolla. John's arms ached slightly from the effort, but he felt lighter, almost refreshed. They pulled their kayaks onto the beach, the sand warm underfoot as they stepped out.

"Thanks for today, Matthew," John said, wiping the salt water from his brow. "I didn't expect a wealth-building session to involve kayaking, but it really helped clear my head."

"Sometimes, getting out into nature can give you the space you need to think," Matthew replied, rolling his shoulders as he pulled the kayak onto the shore. "Besides, the sea caves have a way of putting things into perspective. They've been carved out over millions of years, slowly and steadily—just like how we should approach our financial goals."

John chuckled at the metaphor but nodded in agreement. The ocean breeze tugged at their shirts as they stood there, the sound of distant waves filling the air.

Matthew grabbed his backpack and slung it over his shoulder, preparing to part ways. The late afternoon sun cast a golden hue over the ocean, and a soft breeze drifted between them, carrying with it the sound of distant waves crashing against the shore. He paused for a moment, his gaze steady on John, who stood quietly, arms crossed as if bracing himself for the weight of the conversation.

"Remember, John," Matthew said, breaking the silence and locking eyes with his friend. "The important thing is consistency. Make small, intentional changes and stick with them. It won't always be easy, but it'll be worth it." There was a seriousness in his voice, the kind that came from years of experience and conviction.

John, usually quick with a comment or a joke, found himself nodding, absorbing the words. He extended his hand, gripping Matthew's with a firmness that spoke of gratitude and determination. "I'll keep that in mind. I'll check in with you soon and let you know how I'm doing," he replied.

Matthew's face softened into a broad smile. "Looking forward to it. Oh, and before I go..." He paused for effect, the smile growing wider.

PRELUDE

⤜⤜⤛

(To Chapters 17-21)

"Congratulations, John, for making it this far into our wealth-building sessions. I hope you've learned a few things about cultural interference in wealth building and that you're ready to dive into some foundational concepts that will help you attain your American Dream."

John raised an eyebrow, curiosity piqued. He opened his mouth to respond, but Matthew continued as if needing to get the thoughts out before they left his mind.

"In the past few sessions, we've discussed seven well-established cultural influences affecting our daily lives. They're everywhere—so ingrained in our thinking that we barely notice them anymore. They impact us socially, politically, and economically in ways most people never realize. And the worst part is, because they're so embedded in our culture, we accept them as 'just the way things are.' But the truth is, they hold us back financially. They get in the way of our progress."

John shifted his weight, glancing out at the ocean for a moment. "I get what you're saying, but give me an example. What kind of cultural influence are we talking about here?"

Matthew took a step closer, his expression earnest. "Okay, think about this: you've just moved into a new house, right? You're still trying to pay off some debt, but you also just had a newborn. Suddenly, the financial pressure triples, and you're trying to keep your head above water. That's what I mean by converging events. For the unprepared family, the combination of these life milestones can be financially overwhelming. The stress, the debt, the new responsibilities—it's a recipe for hardship if you're not careful."

John nodded, understanding. "Yeah, I've seen that happen to people I know. Everything hits at once."

"Exactly. And without proper planning, it leads to undesirable outcomes," Matthew said, a note of urgency creeping into his voice. "That's what we're trying to avoid. So, in the next few sessions, we're going to focus on a few basic concepts that might not seem like they relate directly to money—at least not in terms of dollars and cents. But trust me, they do, indirectly. Without a good grasp of these concepts, it's going to be tough to get ahead financially. The goal here is to help you see money differently, to help you understand how to use it to become financially independent."

Matthew reached out and clasped John's shoulder, a silent gesture of encouragement. "You've got this, man. It's all about shifting your perspective. It's not just about making money—it's about how you manage everything else around it."

John exhaled slowly, the enormity of it all sinking in. "I hear you, Matthew. I've already got a lot to think about."

Matthew gave a final nod, offering one last wave as he turned toward the parking lot. "Take it one step at a time. We'll pick up where we left off next time."

John watched him go, the sound of Matthew's footsteps growing fainter with each step. He stood there for a moment, letting the waves and wind fill the silence that had settled around him. His mind was a whirl of thoughts—about the future, about his finances, about the life he wanted to build.

John stood there for a moment, watching Matthew walk away, his mind still processing everything they had talked about. He glanced back out at the ocean, its vastness a reminder of the journey. With a deep breath, he turned and headed toward his own car, already planning the changes he would make in his life.

CHAPTER 17

❧

Money From Heaven

John was excited to arrive at the Compass Balloons. The morning was crisp, with the horizon painted in soft pastels of dawn. The fields were open and sprawling, and in the distance, he could see the brilliant colors of a half-inflated hot air balloon. Matthew stood by the balloon's basket, dressed casually.

"John!" Matthew called out, waving as John approached. The balloon's crew was busy preparing for the flight, but there was a sense of calm efficiency about them. The faint roar of the propane burner echoed as the balloon slowly began to rise upright.

"Matthew, good to see you," John said, extending a hand as they met. "This is quite the way to start a session."

Matthew shook his hand firmly and smiled. "I figured we'd mix things up a bit. The best way to gain perspective is from above, don't you think?" He gestured to the balloon behind him. "We'll have the skies to ourselves today."

The two climbed into the wicker basket as the ground crew gave them the final go-ahead. The balloon began to rise ently, lifting them away from the earth with a smoothness that surprised John.

As they ascended, Cardiff and its surrounding landscape zoomed out beneath them. The fields stretched out like a patchwork quilt, and the coastline shimmered in the distance. The silence was only interrupted by the periodic bursts of the burner, and soon, they were high above the world, floating peacefully.

"Bringing God into a financial course may not appear practical," Matthew said, "It's also risky because you may not even believe He exists. But he is inescapably present in everything we do, including our daily financial affairs."

John turned to look at Matthew. He had heard bits of this perspective before but never in the context of wealth-building.

As the hot air balloon glided smoothly through the sky, Matthew paused for a moment, allowing the vastness of the view to emphasize his next point. The sun had risen higher, casting a golden light across the landscape below. John, absorbed by the sight, listened intently as Matthew continued.

"In our present cultural climate," Matthew continued, "it's easy to undermine the presence of our Creator." He lifted a hand to gesture toward the earth below them. "One reason is that he is invisible in a world that continually demands our attention with various attractions—technology, entertainment, and consumerism. There's always something pulling us away."

John nodded slowly. "It's true. Everything around us feels so immediate, so distracting."

Matthew smiled knowingly. "Exactly. The other reason is that some people find it hard to exercise faith in a culture that demands proof to substantiate reality. If you can't see it, touch it, or measure it, it's hard for many to believe in it."

"But just because something isn't tangible doesn't make it less real," John said, reflecting on the concept.

"Right," Matthew affirmed. "This makes God no less authentic or reachable among the physical clutter that keeps us busy and distracted. He is forever present, all-knowing, and willing to assist those who request his help through faith. And more than that—nothing happens in this world without his knowledge or permission."

John looked down at the miniature world below, contemplating the vastness of what Matthew was saying.

"Think about it," Matthew went on. "He is aware of everything—every bird, every gust of wind, every detail of our lives. And often, He controls both the spiritual and physical events in the universe, including the daily details of our lives."

The balloon floated gently, its path seemingly directed by the invisible currents in the air, reinforcing Matthew's point.

"For these reasons," Matthew said, turning to face John directly, "God can be the perfect companion on your journey through life. He is loving, understanding, compassionate, patient, caring, merciful—and more. With Him by your side, your journey, especially in personal finance, will be more successful and fulfilling."

John remained quiet, absorbing the magnitude of what Matthew was laying out. "How does that translate into finances, though?" he finally asked, curious but respectful.

"Well," Matthew continued, "how he may effectively impact your monetary outcome depends on how well you know him and recognize his influence in your life. Your relationship with God begins by first understanding that he owns everything in the grand scheme of life."

He paused, letting the silence of the skies settle before continuing.

"From his wisdom and power, he formed the universe, including the earth and human life, by simply commanding them into existence. The Bible proclaims, 'For every animal of the forest is mine, and the cattle on a thousand hills. I know every bird in the mountains and the insects in the fields are mine. If I were hungry, I would not tell you, for the world is mine and all that is in it.'" Matthew recited the verse from Psalm 50:10–12 with a quiet reverence.

John listened closely, sensing that Matthew wasn't just reciting words but imparting something deeply personal.

"Now, in that text, God was addressing a problem with ancient Israel regarding animal sacrifices," Matthew explained. "But today, the same could be said about money and other possessions. The idea is that everything we need is a byproduct of the physical world God created—the very produce you eat, the house you occupy, and the materials used to build it."

John's gaze drifted across the landscape, and he could see the logic in Matthew's words. "Like the precious metals we use as commodities," John said, catching on. "Gold, silver, even things like platinum—they all come from the earth."

"Exactly," Matthew nodded. "And God put them there. When you start seeing your wealth—whether it's money, property, or investments—as something entrusted to you by God, it changes your relationship with it. Furthermore, God has endowed individuals with specific abilities and knowledge in physics, chemistry, and other fields of natural science. He gave us the intellect to understand and use the elements of the earth to form the things we need—the desired objects or commodities."

John listened intently, watching as Matthew gestured subtly toward the earth below them.

"Look at everything around us—automobiles, buildings, bridges, airplanes, computers. All of it is possible because God instilled knowledge into humanity, passing it down from generation to generation to ensure our survival and advancement."

John thought about it for a moment. "It's amazing when you put it that way," he said. "We often take these advancements for granted, but they had to start somewhere."

Matthew nodded. "Exactly. And if you feel the urge to succeed in a big way, that ambition isn't an accident. It's not just a human desire—it's a spiritual gift that originated from God."

John glanced at Matthew, processing the idea. He had always felt that his drive for success came from somewhere deep within, but the notion that it was a divine gift gave him a new perspective.

"In addition to giving us ambition," Matthew continued, "God expects us to seek his help when necessary, and he promises to guide us through success. 'I will instruct you and teach you how you should go; I will guide you with my eye.' That's from Psalm 32:8. What a comforting idea, isn't it? To know that your Creator is able, willing, and ready to assist you with your ambitions."

John nodded slowly, the weight of Matthew's words sinking in. "So, it's not just about what I can do on my own... I need to ask for help when I need it."

Matthew turned to face him fully, a reassuring smile on his face. "Yes, I believe it that way. All you have to do is ask. But this promise isn't just for people with ambitious intents—it's for everyone."

He paused, letting the wind carry the silence for a moment before continuing.

"It's for those wise enough to realize they can't control everything in life, who feel humble enough to admit they need help. It's for those who know him as the master of the universe and seek his counsel. And it's for those who dare to pray and seek his guidance continually."

John looked out over the green and orange patch below, feeling a sense of peace as he considered Matthew's words.

"I believe every human being is put on this earth for a purpose," Matthew continued, "One way to discover yours is to pray to God and ask him to guide you through the necessary channels to find it. This may include wanting to be financially successful, from modest wages to working toward financial prosperity."

John considered this. "So, even financial success is part of that purpose?"

Matthew nodded. "Absolutely. Like every human being, you have a great deal of needs—some emotional and spiritual, others physical and financial. These needs will remain constant as you age, but your circumstances will change. And that change will force you to experience new challenges every day."

Matthew turned back toward the horizon, his eyes scanning the endless sky. "Many of these issues will be out of your control, yet somehow, they'll get resolved. Some will be fixed by your own direct involvement. Others will be resolved by divine intervention—specific events that come together in time to solve them."

John looked thoughtful, the idea of divine intervention settling in. "I've heard people call that luck," he said after a moment. Matthew smiled knowingly. "Yes, some people call it luck. Others call it miracles. You, too, will define them in your way. But shortly after these events occur, you may quickly forget them, thinking you have everything under control."

John let out a small chuckle. "That sounds about right."

"Few times, if ever," Matthew said softly, "will you recognize God's mercy on your life? His hand protects you from danger, supplying your needs and guiding you through difficulties. Most people ignore him, but the beauty of it is—God takes no offense when people neglect to recognize his power."

John raised an eyebrow. "He doesn't?"

"No," Matthew said, shaking his head gently. "Although he forgets nothing, he overlooks our careless indiscretions and continues to bless us despite our lack of gratitude. He's just that way."

The balloon's shadow skimmed across the rolling fields as Matthew's voice became more contemplative.

"In your case," Matthew continued, "he is ready to change circumstances in the world to give you favor among people. More specifically, he will provide you with a job to earn an income for shelter, food, clothing, transportation, and more. And while you may think it's all you're doing, he will continue to provide for the things you need."

John was quiet for a moment, absorbing the idea. "He's just... always there."

Matthew smiled warmly. "Yes, he's always there. The Bible says it this way: 'And my God shall supply all your needs according to his riches in glory by Christ Jesus.' That promise is like another verse in Scripture that says, 'He makes his sun rise on the evil and the good and sends rain on the just and the unjust.'"

John looked down at the earth below them, feeling a strange sense of awe.

Matthew continued, "God requires no specific religious belief or personal gratitude to do these things. He does them because he loves us, even when we ignore him."

John exhaled slowly, his mind turning over everything Matthew had said. "That's... a lot to think about."

Matthew smiled, the peacefulness of the moment mirrored in his expression. "It is. But once you start seeing things from this perspective, John, you'll realize you're never truly alone in this journey. There's always someone looking out for you."

The balloon swayed gently as it drifted, and Matthew paused for a moment, looking down at the patchwork of land below them. He took a deep breath as if drawing strength from the stillness before continuing.

"Money," he said thoughtfully, "or wealth, however you choose to call it, is another gift from God. It's not just something we chase or work for on our own. The very means by which we pay for almost everything in life comes from his hand."

John glanced at Matthew, who was now gazing into the horizon, his face illuminated by the soft light of the late morning sun.

"We find direct references in the Bible that show his benevolence," Matthew continued, the wind catching his voice and carrying it gently. "As for every man to whom God has given riches and wealth, and given him the power to eat of it, to receive his heritage, and rejoice in his labor—this is the gift of God.'"

John let the words sink in. The notion that money, something often viewed with cynicism or greed, could be a divine gift was new to him. He had always seen it as something to be earned through hard work, something that was the result of personal effort. Yet, Matthew was suggesting it was something deeper.

"God provides an income," Matthew said, turning slightly toward John. "He gives us the ambition to work, the opportunities to land the right jobs, and even the favor we find among people when we're promoted. He gives us the health to keep working, and with the money we earn, we can obtain the desires of our hearts. But it's not just the money that's important—it's the awareness that it comes from him."

John nodded slowly. "So, recognizing it's a gift from God is the first step to financial success?"

"Exactly," Matthew replied, his tone growing more earnest. "But here's the thing—God's blessings are not always entirely free. Many of them come with stipulations. There's often a kind of exchange. He wants us to reciprocate in kind."

John looked curious. "What kind of exchange are we talking about?"

"At the very least," Matthew explained, "He wants us to recognize his love and kindness with reverence and gratitude. This is how he puts it in Scripture: 'Let not the wise man glory in his wisdom, nor the mighty man glory in his might, nor let the rich man glory in his riches. But let him who glories glory in this: That he understands and knows me; that I am the Lord, exercising loving kindness, judgment, and righteousness in the earth. For in these, I delight,' says the Lord."

Matthew's voice softened as he quoted the text. "It's clear, isn't it? God is the one who bestows goodness on humanity, and he wants us to know it. But he also doesn't want us to get so wrapped up in the gift that we forget the Giver."

John smiled faintly. "That happens a lot, though, doesn't it?"

"It does," Matthew agreed, nodding. "He, too, has needs, though they're simple. He asks for acknowledgment of his goodness, love, and mercy. Those who recognize his benevolence will continue to find favor in his presence, and I hope, John, that you experience that favor soon."

There was a moment of silence between them, broken only by the gentle rush of air as the balloon moved across the sky.

"When donors contribute a certain amount of wealth or assets to an organization or individual, they expect the gift to be used wisely," Matthew continued, turning back toward the horizon. "Strangely enough, God feels the same way."

John raised an eyebrow. "He holds us responsible for using the gifts he gives us?"

"Yes, He holds us accountable," Matthew confirmed. "Especially with money. He expects us to put his blessings—whether it's wealth, talents, or wisdom—to good use. There's a powerful parable that illustrates this point."

John leaned forward slightly, intrigued.

"Jesus once told his disciples a story," Matthew said, his voice lowering as if drawing John into the narrative. "A master was about to embark on a long journey.

Before leaving, he entrusted his wealth to three servants. To one, he gave five bags of gold. To another, two bags. And to the last, one bag. He gave according to each person's ability."

Matthew's eyes flickered with intensity as he recounted the parable. "The servant who received five bags of gold invested it and gained five more. The servant who received two bags did the same, gaining two more. But the servant with one bag—what did he do?"

John's brow furrowed. "He hid it?"

"That's right," Matthew said with a small nod. "He dug a hole and buried the money in the ground. When the master returned, he asked each servant to give an account of what they'd done with the wealth. The first servant presented ten bags of gold, and the master was pleased. 'Well done, good and faithful servant,' he said. 'You were faithful over a few things; I will make you ruler over many things. Enter into the joy of your Lord.' The second servant received the same praise for doubling his share."

"And the third servant?" John asked, already sensing the shift in tone.

Matthew's expression darkened slightly. "The third servant faced the master and said, 'Lord, I knew you to be a hard man, reaping where you have not sown, gathering where you have not scattered seed. I was afraid, so I hid your money. Here, take what is yours.'

The master's response was sharp. 'You wicked and lazy servant. You knew I reap where I have not sown and gather where I have not scattered seed? You should have at least put my money in the bank so I could collect interest.'"

John grimaced. "That's... harsh."

"It's unconventional, yes," Matthew admitted. "But it shows a side of God's justice. While he is loving and merciful, he's also reasonable and just. When we're entrusted with something, he expects us to act responsibly with it."

John was silent, pondering those words.

Matthew's voice softened again. "Our income—what we earn—falls within the framework of God's benevolence. He may not send manna from heaven as he did for the Israelites, but he provides natural resources, opportunities, and the means to earn a living. He promised to meet our needs, and he did. All he asks in return is gratitude."

Matthew turned to John, his eyes serious but kind. "And that gratitude involves reverence, John. It's a simple but profound way to acknowledge the Giver and to keep the blessings flowing in your life."

As the hot air balloon gently descended, the landscape below came into sharper focus. The distant hills that seemed so vast from above now appeared smaller, and the earthy scent of the ground rose to greet them as the balloon slowly approached its landing.

Matthew, still gazing toward the horizon, spoke with a calm conviction.

"When God supplies your needs," he began, his voice steady as the basket swayed slightly, "he expects you to be a good steward of what he provides. This isn't just about money—it relates to all aspects of your life—but especially in the area of personal finance."

John listened closely, the steady rhythm of the wind and the soft hiss of the balloon's burner framing the words.

"If you believe that your income is truly a gift from God," Matthew continued, turning his head to meet John's eyes, "you'll treat it with utmost respect. You'll think twice before squandering your salary on things that are fleeting, things that bring no lasting value."

The balloon touched down lightly, and the gentle thump was a reminder of their descent from the peaceful sky back to the reality of the ground. As the pilot worked to secure the basket, Matthew pressed on.

"Think about it this way," he said, leaning forward slightly, "carelessly spending your income is like watching the money go up in smoke—or flushing it down the toilet. It's a practice that shows a disregard for the blessings you've been given."

John nodded thoughtfully, reflecting on his spending habits. He had never thought of it that way before.

Matthew's tone grew more serious. "Imagine having a financial plan that doesn't include savings or investment. That's like the trustee who dug a hole and buried his master's money in the ground. He didn't lose it outright, but he certainly didn't do anything to make it grow. And the result? Predictably disappointing—not just for the master but for the trustee as well."

The wind picked up slightly, causing the balloon to sway again as the crew began to tether it down securely. Matthew smiled gently at John.

"I hope, John, that as you move forward, you'll include God in your financial aspirations. If you do, he will guide you toward prosperity—not just materially, but in all aspects of your life."

John met Matthew's gaze with understanding. "As you work with him, you'll start to see changes—not just in how you handle your money, but in how you handle everything in your life. Responsibility comes with time and trust. The more you trust him, the more responsible you'll become with all the gifts he's given you."

By now, the balloon had fully landed, and the crew was preparing for their disembarkation. The breeze carried the scent of freshly cut grass and wildflowers, and the late morning sky was painted in a bright shade of blue.

They stepped out of the basket, feet back on solid ground, yet John felt like he was carrying something new with him—something intangible but powerful. The wind tousled their hair as they made their way to the side of the field where a car was waiting. Matthew extended his hand to John with a smile. "Until next time?"

John shook his hand firmly. "Yeah, definitely. I'm looking forward to it."

As they parted ways, John felt more clarity. The flight had been more than just a breathtaking view—it had been an elevation of his understanding, a conversation that would stay with him long after their next session. Matthew turned back for a moment, calling out over the sound of the wind, "Remember, John—prosperity isn't just about what you gain. It's about how you manage what you've been given."

John smiled and waved, knowing those words would echo in his mind as he drove home.

CHAPTER 18

❧

The Economy: A Friend Or Foe?

Matthew and John settled into their seats at Petco Park as fans slowly trickled in, filling the stadium with excitement. The scent of popcorn and hot dogs wafted through the air, and the vibrant buzz of chatter and music filled the atmosphere. John looked around, taking in the crowd and the energy, then turned to Matthew.

"I didn't know you were into sports," John said with a grin. "I figured you were all business."

Matthew leaned back in his seat, casually adjusting his cap as he gazed out at the field. "Oh, I love sports," he replied, "It's all about strategy, really. You get to see how teams work together, the dynamics between players, and, of course, how they all aim to win. It's not so different from building wealth when you think about it."

John chuckled, nodding as he sipped his drink. "I guess you can find lessons anywhere."

Matthew smiled, then shifted the conversation seamlessly into their wealth-building session. "Speaking of lessons, as you work toward financial freedom, it's essential to understand how the economy works. And don't worry—no complicated jargon today." He leaned in slightly, his tone growing more focused. "In this session, you'll get a basic understanding of the system, and trust me, this will be critical for your future success."

Just as Matthew began to explain, the stadium erupted into cheers as the San Diego Padres took the field. The crowd rose to its feet in a wave of applause, and the noise was electric. Matthew paused, letting the excitement wash over them before continuing with his lesson.

"Alright," he said with a smile once the roar died down. "So, what is the economy? In a real sense, it's like this ballpark. It pulls people together—everyone from the players on the field to the vendors selling drinks and snacks. They're all here, participating and contributing to the event. The economy works much the same way, bringing people and resources together for enterprising events."

John nodded, glancing around the stadium, seeing it now through Matthew's analogy. "So, like a giant playing field?"

"Yes, John," Matthew confirmed. "It's the playing field where all business activities happen. It involves people's talents, like the labor you see from these workers, raw materials like the equipment they use, and of course, capital—money to fund it all."

The game began, and the crowd surged with another wave of cheers as the first pitch was thrown. John watched for a moment, but his focus was still on Matthew's words.

"With this mix of talent, resources, and money, entrepreneurs create goods and services for people. And here's the key," Matthew continued, "nothing happens outside the economy in the world of business. We often talk about 'The Economy' as if it's some separate, living thing, but really, it's just us—people like you and me—doing business, trading, and working."

John's eyes followed the action on the field, but he was clearly digesting Matthew's words. "So, it needs us to function."

"Exactly," Matthew nodded. "It's not alive on its own. It depends on human involvement to keep it going. Picture the economy as a worldwide commercial playground. People are out there transacting business 24/7, providing goods and services, and making profits."

Matthew gestured to the field, where the players were fully engaged in their own high-stakes game. "Take Wall Street, for example. People think it's the heart of the US economy, but in reality, it's just one small part. The economy isn't limited to a few blocks in New York. It's in every state, every city, and even here in Petco Park. Each one of us plays a role."

John nodded slowly, his eyes narrowing as he considered the broader implications. "So, every time I pay for something—whether it's rent, gas, or even a coffee—I'm participating in the economy?"

"That's right," Matthew said, leaning forward slightly as the crowd erupted in applause for a successful play on the field. "When you buy your daily latte, you're part of the system. And the person who made that latte? They're in it too. Every day, we contribute to this massive, interconnected system through our labor, our money, and our purchases."

A crack of the bat echoed through the stadium as a line drive shot through the infield, sending the crowd into a frenzy. Matthew paused to let the excitement pass, then continued.

"The thing is, this didn't always exist like it does now. Centuries ago, we had a bartering system. People exchanged goods and services directly—like trading bread for wool. However, over time, we needed more flexibility, which led to the use of cash and, eventually, to the more complex system we have today. Entrepreneurs were the key drivers of that evolution. When entrepreneurs invest cash in a building to establish a medical facility and hire people to care for the sick, they participate in the economy. When a plumber comes to your house to fix a problem and receives payment for the service, they also participate in the economy. When these and other activities are put in motion and multiplied throughout the country, the economy is essentially active."

John glanced around at the sea of fans, each of them involved in their own way, whether as workers, vendors, or simply spectators enjoying the game. "It's hard to imagine it starting so simple," he said.

Matthew smiled, eyes twinkling with amusement. "It's grown into something far beyond simple. Today, every nation on earth has an economy, and all these microeconomies contribute to the larger global system. Through trade, nations benefit from one another's resources and skills."

John's eyes followed a vendor making his way up the stairs, balancing a tray of snacks as he weaved through the crowd. "So, everything we see here— every job, every transaction—is part of that bigger picture?"

"Exactly," Matthew said. "And once you understand how it all works, you can start to see how to navigate it better—how to use the system to your advantage. That's what we'll be focusing on as we continue."

The game progressed, the energy of the crowd ebbing and flowing like a tide, but John's mind remained fixed on the intricate systems Matthew had begun to unravel for him.

"See," Matthew said, "whether it was weak or strong, the economy had to keep moving. It's like this game—no matter the score, the players keep playing. Sure, governments can restrict economic activities for a time, like during a crisis, but if that lasts too long, the whole system starts to fall apart. That's why it seems like the economy has a life of its own."

John, chewing on a pretzel, glanced at Matthew. "Yeah, I've heard people say the economy is like a living thing. But I guess it makes sense—if people stop trading, everything collapses."

"Exactly," Matthew nodded. "The economy was born from basic human needs—survival, growth—and it would keep going as long as humanity existed. But at its core, the system was pretty simple: it was all about taking and giving."

The buzz of the crowd had faded for a moment as the Padres stepped up to bat again, the players poised in anticipation. Matthew used the pause in the game to continue his lesson.

"Let's say an entrepreneur has an idea for a business," Matthew began. "They might have the vision, but they can't do it all themselves. They need people—skilled workers for marketing, research, finance, whatever the business requires."

John nodded thoughtfully, cutting in. "I get that. In our real estate business, we had to bring in other agents, accountants, and marketers. You can't scale without a solid team."

Matthew smiled, acknowledging John's insight. "Exactly. The entrepreneur's first contribution to the economy is hiring and investing in people, equipment, and capital to get things running. Now, think of this happening on a global scale—entrepreneurs everywhere starting businesses, hiring, and injecting money into the economy."

John shifted in his seat, his gaze scanning the crowd. "It's not like I haven't seen this before," he said, his voice reflecting a deep understanding. "But the way you're framing it... the scale of it, how each individual decision ripples out—that's what's hitting me differently."

Matthew caught the subtle shift in John's tone. "It's that larger system at work. You and I, and everyone else with a job, we're part of this massive system. We provide our skills and labor, and in return, the economy gives us something—our paychecks. The cycle begins when we spend that money on goods and services."

John's expression softened as he reconsidered. "Yeah, I've always understood the business part, but I see now that it's part of something much bigger than I gave it credit for."

A cheer had erupted as the batter swung and connected with the ball, sending it soaring into the outfield. Matthew and John, along with the rest of the crowd, jumped to their feet, shouting their approval as the ball landed in the stands. The noise swelled, but as the excitement faded, Matthew continued.

"So, the economy takes an investment of capital from entrepreneurs and gives back profits, most of the time. For people like us, it takes our labor and gives us wages or salaries. But the system needs something else to keep it going—spending."

"Spending, sure," John said, not surprised. "I've seen it firsthand in our business. People get a paycheck and almost immediately funnel it back into the economy, whether it's through home purchases, dining out, or even investments."

Matthew nodded. "Exactly. It's not enough for people to just make money. The system thrives on spending. Every time we buy something—food, gas, or tickets to a Padres game—we're feeding the system. That's how the cycle completes itself."

John took a sip of his drink, digesting the information. "It's crazy to think that everything we do—work, spending, all of it—keeps this massive system going."

Matthew chuckled. "It is, but that's how it works. And here's where things get interesting. When you look at the economy as a living entity, you start to see how it's a little manipulative."

John's brow furrowed. "What do you mean?"

Matthew turned to face him, his voice steady. "Salaries and wages, for instance. Apart from a few top executives making ridiculous sums of money, the economy limits most of us. It does this through job classifications. Engineers make around the same salary. Teachers, too. Same for mechanics, programmers, soldiers, truck drivers—the system imposes pay restrictions on us."

John had frowned, thinking. "I've noticed that. In my field, most people get paid about the same unless they've got more experience or extra qualifications."

"Exactly," Matthew said. "That's how the system controls compensation. Sure, it gives you a job, but it also tells you, 'If you perform this specific function, you'll earn this much and no more.' So, if you want to make more, what do you do?"

John sat back, arms crossed, pondering. "Well, I guess you'd have to get more education or more experience either or just get another job in a different industry, right?"

The stadium roared again as a Padres player rounded the bases, and Matthew let the excitement wash over them before continuing. "But even then," Matthew said, "they're going to run into the same income restrictions." He paused, glancing at John to make sure the point was sinking in. "The bottom line is this: if you rely on a job or career for your income, know that your income will be permanently fixed."

John looked skeptical, his brow furrowing. "Permanently?"

"Yes," Matthew nodded, "No matter how much money you make, your wants and desires will always outpace your income. That's just how it works."

John sat back, crossing his arms as he mulled over the statement. The crowd around them was erupting in cheers, but Matthew pressed on.

"This creates one of the greatest financial challenges we face. We often ignore the limits of our income and instead focus on satisfying our wants—spending too much in the process. That's where people get into trouble, with debt piling up and finances spinning out of control."

"So, you're saying no matter what, we'll never have enough?" John asked, taking a long drink from his soda, his eyes narrowing in thought.

"Not quite," Matthew replied, "but unless you're incredibly wealthy, your desires will always exceed what you can afford. And even for the super-rich, there are always things money can't buy. It's a cycle that feeds itself. As our income increases, so do our desires for more things. If you don't manage it, this can drive you crazy."

John shifted uncomfortably in his seat. "So what's the solution?"

"The solution is simple but not always easy. You have to learn to live within your means. Make do with less, not more. The sooner you start doing that, the faster you'll reach financial independence."

John nodded slowly, still digesting the idea. The Padres made a double play on the field, and the crowd erupted into applause, but it was background noise to their conversation now.

"There's something else," Matthew continued, his voice lowering slightly, almost conspiratorial. "Most of us overlook an important aspect of the economy—the idea of vanishing income. You see, the economy can take back everything it gives you without you even realizing it."

John's brow furrowed again. "What do you mean?"

"Let's say you get a paycheck," Matthew explained, using his hands for emphasis. "It represents 100% of your salary, right? Now, if you spend the entire amount—on groceries, bills, entertainment—by the end of the month, the economy has taken back 100% of that paycheck."

John blinked, and the realization started to hit. "So... you're left with nothing?"

"Exactly," Matthew said. "All your cash is gone, and you're left with two options: either stop spending until your next paycheck arrives or fall back on credit to keep shopping."

"And most people fall back on credit, don't they?" John asked knowingly, already predicting the answer.

"Unfortunately, yes," Matthew said, sighing. "That's where most people get outwitted by the economy. They don't wait for the next paycheck. They rely on credit, and it becomes a vicious cycle. The economy gives you an income, but if you let it, it'll take everything back. It's like watching your money vanish into thin air."

John rubbed his temples. "So how do you stop it?"

Matthew leaned forward, his tone becoming more intense. "The key is not to let the economy take back 100% of your paycheck. You have to save some of it, no matter what. If you spend everything you earn, you'll be cash-poor and in debt for the rest of your life. Your first and most important goal should be to save a portion of your income every month."

John nodded, already familiar with the concept. "I've been putting money aside for a while now—mostly for investments and a rainy day fund. But how much are we talking about here? I'm curious to hear your take."

Matthew smiled, appreciating the question. "Ideally, you shouldn't spend more than 80% of your income on living expenses. The remaining 20% should be split: 10% goes toward wealth-building, and 10% goes into an emergency fund. It's a simple formula but incredibly powerful. When you start banking some of your paychecks each month, you're using the system in your favor."

John considered it, intrigued but not unfamiliar. "I've been saving consistently, but hearing you break it down that way makes me wonder if I've been optimizing my approach. So by sticking to those percentages, you're saying I can turn the system to my advantage even more?"

Matthew chuckled. "In a way, yes. When you save strategically, the economy becomes a friend. It rewards you with greater wealth over time. But if you let it, the economy can become a foe, constantly draining your finances because you didn't control the flow."

John smirked. "Sounds like a game I've been playing, but maybe it's time to play it smarter."

As the final out was called, the crowd at Petco Park roared to life, their cheers echoing through the stadium as the San Diego Padres secured the win. Fireworks lit up the night sky, and fans erupted in celebration. Matthew and John stood up, stretching after the long game. The excitement of the evening was still buzzing around them, but their conversation had left an even stronger impression.

Matthew clapped John on the shoulder, smiling. "Well, that was a solid game. Glad we could catch it."

John grinned back. "Yeah, it was a good one. I have to admit, I didn't expect you to be into baseball like this."

"Surprises never hurt," Matthew chuckled, glancing around at the throngs of people filing out of the stands. "It's nice to unwind, but remember, we've got more important things to cover next week."

John nodded, "Yeah, I'm still wrapping my head around what we talked about tonight. There's a lot I need to work on, especially about not letting the economy take back everything I earn."

"That's the step," Matthew said as they began to walk toward the exit. "And next week, we'll dive into some practical strategies for wealth-building. You're doing great so far, John. It's all about steady progress."

John smiled, a hint of determination flashing in his eyes. "Looking forward to it.'

The warm San Diego night greeted them as they stepped out of the stadium, the sky a deep purple with city lights twinkling in the distance. The post-game chatter of fans filled the air.

Matthew extended his hand, and John shook it firmly. "Same time next week?" Matthew asked.

"Absolutely," John replied. "I'll be ready."

They exchanged a final nod before parting ways. John watched as Matthew disappeared into the crowd, his mind already racing with thoughts of their next session.

CHAPTER 19

❧

Stretching the Dollar

As John and Matthew stood at the edge of Point Loma, the Pacific waves crashing against the rugged cliffs below, the golden hues of the setting sun reflected off the water. The wind was gentle, carrying the smell of salt and the distant sounds of seabirds.

John inhaled deeply, appreciating the tranquility of the moment, before Matthew broke the silence.

"In business management school," Matthew began, his eyes on the horizon, "students are taught that there are limits to all things."

John nodded, his gaze still fixed on the ocean. "It's true," he said. "In real estate, you see it all the time. Land is finite; opportunities are finite...but it's not something most people think about."

"Exactly," Matthew continued. "The concept goes beyond just business—it touches everything in life. The lives of animals, plants, and even people have beginnings and endings. Eventually, we all disappear into the unknown, never to be seen again. It's the same with resources, like the land and water around us. They're limited to what is known to exist on Earth. The same can be said for the sand on the beaches and the trees on this planet. The list can go on."

John glanced over, raising an eyebrow. "What are you getting at?"

Matthew leaned forward slightly, resting his hands on the rail. "Understanding limits in our universe is crucial for success in any endeavor. In business, in government operations, in science—every field. And most people, even those who manage these things every day, don't fully grasp it."

John thought for a moment. "So you're saying people waste resources because they don't respect those limits?"

Matthew nodded. "Yes. Think about it: those who understand limits are highly valued. They're often called the 'guardians of resources.' They know how to use what they've been given—whether it's money, equipment, or employees—and ensure they last. On the other hand, those who don't get it? They burn through resources as if more will magically appear. But it doesn't. Somehow, they never seem to have enough to complete their tasks promptly and efficiently."

John chuckled softly. "Sounds a lot like my past self and some of the people I've worked with."

Matthew smiled. "It's a universal problem. And it doesn't just apply to business. Think about your home, about money. The dollar is a finite resource, too. And yet, how often do people live as if it's limitless?"

John shifted his stance, folding his arms as he listened. "True. It's easy to get caught up in that cycle, spending before thinking."

As the sky above Point Loma transitioned from shades of bright pink to orange, Matthew leaned against a weathered railing, his voice calm but firm. "This means accepting that the dollar is a finite commodity," he said, watching the horizon, "one that can stretch only so far before it breaks."

John, who had been silent, had his arms crossed as he looked out toward the ocean, tilting his head slightly. "We all know money has limits," he said. "But we don't always act like it."

Matthew nodded, turning to face him. "From an educational standpoint, we get it. We're reminded of it every time our bank accounts run dry, every time we have to wait for the next paycheck to cover bills." He paused, letting the words sink in. "But behaviorally? It's a different story. People act as though their money supply never ends, spending beyond what they have as if there's always more to tap into."

John let out a soft chuckle. "You're not wrong. I've seen people, including myself, who go on spending sprees the moment they get a credit card as if it's free money. And then, they're stuck paying for it months, even years later."

"Exactly," Matthew agreed, his tone more serious now. "That's the paradox. Intellectually, we know money is limited, yet we spend like it isn't.

This happens on every level, not just individuals. Corporations, governments, even entire countries fall into this trap."

John leaned in, intrigued. "How so?"

"Take government revenue," Matthew explained. "Each year, the government collects taxes, right? That revenue is limited by what they collect. Yet federal and state lawmakers create budgets that exceed those amounts year after year. Why? Because they're spending on things they can't afford—new obligations, runaway programs. The problem is, they don't stop. Instead, they push the burden onto taxpayers, whether they support the spending or not."

John's brow furrowed. "So, it's like they're playing with other people's money."

"Exactly," Matthew continued. "And businesses do it too. When managers ignore solid financial practices, they run into cash-flow problems. Maybe they overestimate revenue, or maybe they don't account for operating costs. It doesn't matter if they've got the best product on the market—if they run out of money, the business suffers. You can't operate without cash."

John ran a hand through his hair. "I've seen that happen. Great ideas, terrible management. They never last."

Matthew leaned closer, his voice quiet but commanding. "And here's the thing—what's true for governments and businesses is just as true for households. Your home is a microeconomic system bound by the same financial principles. The only real difference is scale."

John raised an eyebrow. "You're saying my home is like a business?"

'In many ways, yes," Matthew replied. "Just like a business, your household generates revenue—only, instead of selling goods or services, you trade your time and skills for income. The money that comes into your home operates under the same principles as corporate revenue. And just like a business, if you mismanage your finances, you'll run into cash-flow issues."

John let that sink in for a moment. "But most people think business finance is a whole different world. You know, more complicated."

Matthew shrugged. "It's more complex because of the scale—the amount of money and the number of activities involved. But at its core, it's the same. The exact dollar that flows through a government or business also flows through your home. The same accounting principles apply. If you overspend at home, just like in business, there will be consequences."

John sighed, a small smile creeping onto his face. "So, what you're saying is my house is a small business, and I'm its CEO?"

Matthew chuckled softly. "In a way, yes. You're managing resources, balancing income and expenses, and making financial decisions that affect everyone in your household. The only real difference is the terminology—what a business calls revenue, you call income. But it's all the same money. And it can all run out if you're not careful."

John scratched his chin, the weight of Matthew's words pressing on him. "Never thought of it that way before. Makes sense, though."

As the glow of the setting sun painted over them, creating long shadows across the cliffs of Point Loma, Matthew glanced at John, gauging his reaction before pressing on. "The ongoing notion," Matthew said, "is that the tools necessary for managing government and business finances don't apply to the home. But let's be honest, that's far from true."

John shifted slightly, leaning on the railing, the distant sound of crashing waves below a soothing backdrop to their conversation. "You're saying people should treat their personal finances like a business or a government budget, except for the part where they overspend?" he asked, intrigued.

Matthew smiled faintly. "That's exactly what I'm saying. Think about it—how many people actually use a budget in their personal lives? Statistically, most of us know we should, and we even encourage others to do it, but few follow through. Instead, we rely on memory and impulse to manage our money, and that's a dangerous game."

John chuckled. "I've been guilty of that more times than I'd like to admit. It's easy to think you've got it all in your head, but then something comes up, and suddenly you're scrambling."

"Exactly," Matthew said, his tone growing more serious. "Why do you think so many people don't use a budget? Is it that they don't know how? Or do they feel restricted by it? Maybe they think it's unnecessary, or perhaps they lack the discipline to stick with it."

John nodded slowly, considering the questions. "I think it's a little bit of everything. People don't want to feel controlled by a budget, and they definitely don't want to face the reality of their financial situation. It's easier to ignore it."

Matthew's gaze fixed on the horizon, where the sun was lowering below the waterline. "But here's the problem—without a budget, how can we truly understand the limits of money? Financial management can't be done in your head. You can't see the bigger picture without putting numbers on paper or a spreadsheet.'

John turned toward him, "I guess that's where most people stumble. They don't want to take that first step."

"Right," Matthew agreed. "And because of that, they end up in financial trouble. They don't know what's happening with their money, so they stretch it until it breaks. That's why so many people are struggling. They don't have a clear picture of their finances, so they keep making the same mistakes."

John frowned slightly. "So, what's the solution? Just...make a budget and stick to it?"

Matthew smiled knowingly. "It's simpler than people think. One of the easiest ways to avoid financial trouble is to create a budget and use it consistently. And I'm not talking about a one-off plan that you make once and forget about. I mean building a system that works for you. It doesn't matter if you make $30,000 a year or $300,000. When you write it down, you can see how far your income will go before you spend a dime of it."

John raised an eyebrow. "But most people think budgets are too restrictive."

"That's the common misconception," Matthew replied. "But in reality, a budget gives you freedom— it gives you control. It's not about restricting yourself; it's about making informed decisions. For example, if your monthly income is $5,000, you can allocate every dollar with purpose. Maybe you set aside $300 for savings, a deliberate choice that sets you up for financial growth."

Matthew paused, watching the waves roll onto the shore below, their rhythm soothing and timeless. "When you build a budget, you have to keep a few things in mind," he continued. "First, create it for twelve consecutive months, updating it annually. Make sure the model suits your personality—something you'll actually use. Always be aware that your income and expenses might fluctuate from month to month. The important thing is that you have a steady flow of income to cover those changes."

John rubbed his chin thoughtfully. "So, it's not about being rigid. It's about having a plan that adjusts to real life."

"Exactly," Matthew said, nodding. "Once you've built your budget, use it regularly. Twice a month works well for most people. And don't be afraid to create additional columns for specific scenarios—like estimating versus actual spending. That's how you stay on top of your finances."

John's gaze softened as he absorbed the information. "It makes sense. But what about people who say a budget doesn't work for them?"

Matthew chuckled lightly. "A budget is only a tool— it's not the magic solution. The numbers on paper are only half the battle. The other part is you. As you shop or make decisions, you have to exercise control. This means that you must stay within the allotted portion that you set aside for clothing, food, and entertainment. You need to stick to the limits you've set for yourself. If you keep spending beyond your budget, it won't matter how good your plan is—it'll be useless."

John sighed, "I've been there. Overspending, then wondering why I'm not making any progress."

Matthew's voice softened, "It's common, John. A lot of people find themselves in that cycle. But once you get into the habit of using your budget, you'll come to depend on it. You'll keep using it until money is no longer a concern. And even then, you'll still find it invaluable."

John straightened, "So, it's about discipline, isn't it?"

"Exactly," Matthew affirmed. "Discipline and consistency. If you can master those, a budget will become one of your most powerful tools. And when you combine that with the right financial mindset, you'll see the results. *Financial security isn't about how much you make—it's about how well you manage what you have.*"

The wind blew softly as the sky above darkened, the stars beginning to twinkle faintly. John let out a deep breath, feeling Matthew's words settle into him. "Alright, I'll build the budget. Use it about twice a month or every pay period, right?

Matthew smiled, clapping John on the shoulder. "Use it twice a month or on paydays. And don't forget to stick to it."

John nodded, "Yeah, I won't."

Matthew's voice was calm but firm, making sure he had John's full attention. "When people struggle with managing their finances," he began, "they often look for excuses, trying to rationalize why things aren't working out. And more often than not, they blame their low income, claiming they don't make enough money. But here's the reality: that's seldom the true problem."

John crossed his arms, intrigued though a bit skeptical. "If not income, then what is it?" he asked, shifting slightly in his chair.

Matthew's gaze was steady, and his expression was thoughtful. He replied, "It's all about how you manage what you have. Let me give you a couple of scenarios." He leaned back, setting the stage. "Imagine a family that brings home $100,000 a year. Out of that, they spend 20% on nonessential items, 80% on necessities, and save nothing. Now, who should be blamed for their financial problems? The lack of income or poor spending choices?"

John smirked, already sensing the answer. "Definitely poor spending choices."

"Exactly," Matthew nodded. "Now, let's look at another family. They bring home $60,000 a year but manage to save $12,000 of it—20%—while running their household with the rest. Who should be commended for their achievement?"

"The second family, of course. They're saving and managing with less," John said.

"Right again," Matthew continued. "So, based on these two cases, which family do you think will be better off financially by the end of the year? The one making more money, or the one making less but saving?"

John chuckled softly. "The family making less but saving. It's clear."

Matthew leaned forward again, emphasizing his next point. "That's where most people get it wrong. They think financial success is tied to how much they make, but in truth, it's about how much they keep and how wisely they manage what they have. The family making $60,000 with savings will always be better off than the one making $100,000 but saving nothing."

John tapped his chin, reflecting on his own financial choices. "I guess we fall into that trap sometimes—thinking more money will fix everything."

"It's an easy trap to fall into," Matthew agreed. "But as I said earlier in this session, seven cultural issues hold people back from making progress financially. And while all of that is important, the fact remains—you and I are ultimately responsible for our own financial success or failure. We all have the power to make decisions that shape our financial destiny."

John sighed, nodding. "It's tempting, though. There's always something new to buy or keep up with."

"Yes, John," Matthew said, "But even though we're tempted to buy things, the truth is, we don't have to. Just because someone else is making certain financial decisions doesn't mean we need to follow their habits. We have the power to make different choices, smarter choices."

He paused for a moment, letting his words sink in before continuing, "So, if you really want to succeed financially, you'll do whatever it takes to make it happen. And that could be something as simple as implementing a budget for your household finances."

John nodded, a determined look crossing his face. "A budget... It's basic but effective."

"It is," Matthew said with a smile. "And when you use a budget, you begin to appreciate the value of cash. More importantly, it reminds you of the limits of your income. The dollar is a finite resource. It can only stretch so far, and if you spend beyond those limits, it's only a matter of time before you run into trouble."

John uncrossed his arms, leaning forward slightly. "So, what do you recommend?"

Matthew was ready. "If you don't already have a budget, start one today. It'll help you in ways you can't imagine." He counted on his fingers, listing each benefit. "A budget will help you appreciate your income, realize the limits of your cash, and establish boundaries for your spending. It'll also help you start building savings, which will put you at ease and boost your self-esteem. Most importantly, it'll put you in control of your finances."

John nodded slowly, absorbing it all. "And you're saying this is the key to financial success?"

Matthew smiled warmly. "It's not the only key, but it's a major one. A simple budget can do so much good. You'll be surprised at how much more empowered you feel once you start using one. It's about control, John. When you control your money, you control your future."

John glanced at his watch, then back at Matthew. "You've given me a lot to think about. I'm definitely starting a budget when I get home."

"That's great to hear," Matthew said, offering his hand. "Stick with it, and I'm sure you'll see the difference."

John shook Matthew's hand, "I will. And let's meet up again next week for the next session. I want to keep building on this."

"Absolutely," Matthew agreed with a grin. "Next week it is. We'll dig deeper into wealth-building strategies. Until then, stay disciplined and keep making those smart choices."

They parted ways with a sense of purpose; the waves crashing against the cliffs below reminded him of the steady and unrelenting nature of time—just like their financial discipline needed to be.

CHAPTER 20

❧

Five Functions Of Money

As they approached the Davis-Horton House, Matthew and John took in the charm of the historic building. The white façade stood out against the backdrop of the busy Gaslamp Quarter, and its Victorian architecture reminded them of bygone times. The wrought-iron gate creaked as they walked through, and the sound of their footsteps echoed on the old wooden porch. John ran his hand along the railing, his gaze sweeping over the detailed window frames and intricately designed roof.

"This is the oldest structure in the Gaslamp Quarter," Matthew said, "A living artifact from a different time. Imagine life back in 1850 when this house was pre-fabricated in Maine and then shipped around Cape Horn to settle here in San Diego."

John whistled softly. "Hard to believe a house like this made it all the way here in one piece."

Matthew nodded. "Well, back then, the idea of setting up a house in a new land meant thinking long-term. Much like what we're here to discuss today—building a lasting financial foundation."

They entered the museum, greeted by the subtle scent of aged wood and the quiet hum of history preserved in every corner. The guide's voice faded as the two men stood in a corner room.

Matthew started as they sat down at an old wooden table, the kind that might have once held family dinners or important discussions in this very house. "For most people," he said, "the definition of money management involves two essential functions: *income and expenses*."

John listened intently, nodding along as Matthew's words drew him in.

"Money comes in, and money goes out through expenditures. It's a routine most people are stuck in—waiting for that next paycheck to cover rent, food, and utilities until, before they know it, everything's gone. And then, the cycle repeats." Matthew paused, giving John a moment to absorb its gravity.

"It's an exhausting loop," John agreed, leaning back. "But it's hard to break free from."

"Exactly." Matthew's eyes gleamed with the passion of someone who had long escaped that loop. "With that mindset, money becomes just a commodity—something to be spent, nothing more. Now, imagine if everyone thought like that. There would be no savings and no investments. People would lose the drive to dream. The economy? It would crawl. The future would be bleak."

John raised an eyebrow. "But there's got to be more, right?"

Matthew smiled, leaning forward as he spoke. "Of course. Fortunately, the functions of money extend beyond just income and expenses. That's where the real control comes in. Personal finance isn't just about what you earn and what you spend. There are five key elements that make up a complete financial cycle: income, expenses, assets, liability, and equity."

John frowned, the weight of the terms hitting him. "Equity...? So, it's about balance?"

"Yes, each function depends on the other. When you spend money, it affects your liabilities. When you invest in assets, you build equity. The key to financial success is learning how to use these functions together, maximizing control over your money."

As they continued talking, the museum seemed to fade into the background, the relics of the past blending seamlessly with Matthew's forward-thinking insights.

Matthew carefully leaned back in his chair, "This is just an introduction, John. Soon, we'll dive deeper into what I call 'My Hidden Wealth Building Process.' That's where you'll learn how some of the wealthiest people in the world not only build but protect their wealth."

John sat quietly for a moment. He glanced around at the historic room they were in—a room that had seen so much time pass and yet remained standing, solid, preserved.

"Kind of like this house, isn't it?" John said thoughtfully. "Built with foresight, sent on a long journey, and still standing."

Matthew smiled. "Exactly, John. Exactly. Incoming money, John, is the 1st and most essential function," Matthew began, his voice calm but firm. "Without it, everything else would crumble. Income is more than a paycheck—it's the fuel that powers the engine of your personal and professional life."

John tilted his head slightly. "So, it's not just about working a nine-to-five?"

"Exactly," Matthew nodded, a small smile playing at the corners of his mouth. "Think broader. Income includes any money you receive—profits from a business, tips, interest from your savings, dividends, tax refunds, and even insurance payouts or lottery winnings. These are all sources of income. They may be irregular or unexpected, but they're all part of the bigger picture. It's what makes commerce meaningful, what allows government and business operations to function."

John glanced out the window, where the modern city skyline of San Diego stood in sharp contrast to the Victorian architecture of the Gaslamp Museum. "You're right. Without income, personal dreams would just... dangle."

"Hopelessly," Matthew affirmed. "And we rely on it for everything. Paying bills, covering credit card debts, funding dreams...it's the heartbeat of finance."

John sat back, rubbing his chin. "But it's also the easiest part to think about. People know they need money coming in, but what happens when that's all they think about?"

"That's the problem," Matthew continued. "When people only focus on income and expenses—just two functions—they're trapped. They earn, they spend, they wait for the next paycheck, and they repeat. No long-term vision. They'll survive, sure. But they won't thrive."

John's eyes narrowed. "Sounds like a lot of people."

"Far too many," Matthew agreed. "Expenses, the second function, represent the negative outflow—money leaving your hands and going to someone else. It's necessary, but if it's all you focus on, it creates a cycle of spending without saving, investing, or growing. Money just passes through you, like water through a sieve. It leaves you with no financial security."

John let out a low whistle. "And so people can get stuck in that paycheck-to-paycheck loop."

"Exactly." Matthew's voice softened, "Without understanding the other functions—liabilities, assets, and equity—people will keep living for the next paycheck. No growth. No progress."

The sound of soft footsteps echoed down the museum hall, blending with the historical ambiance as Matthew transitioned to the next point.

"Liability is the third function, and it's one that people don't often think about at home," he said. "We tend to associate it with businesses or corporations. But liability affects us all, especially when we take on debt. Car loans, mortgages, even credit card debt—they're all liabilities. If you owe someone money, that's a liability."

John nodded thoughtfully.

Matthew agreed. "You can't ignore it. Any debt means you owe someone, and they have the right to collect. But then, there's the opposite—assets."

"Assets are the good stuff, right?" John smirked.

Matthew chuckled. "Exactly. The fourth function, assets, represents the positive side. Your house, your car, jewelry, investments—these are all assets. They're what you own, and they're your tools for building wealth. Assets are the key to moving beyond the paycheck-to-paycheck mindset."

"And what about equity?" John asked, his curiosity piqued.

Matthew tapped the table lightly. "Equity, the fifth function, is neutral—it's your scorecard. It shows how you're doing financially at any given moment. Are you in the red or the black? Equity tallies it all—your assets, your liabilities—and tells you where you stand. It's how you measure progress."

John sat quietly for a moment, staring at the table as if weighing each function in his mind. "So, how do these five functions work together?"

"Yes," Matthew replied. "Each one influences the other. Neglect one, and it throws off the balance. Use them wisely, and you'll have control over your financial future."

Matthew glanced at his watch, "We're nearing the end of this session, but we'll dive deeper into these concepts in our next few meetings. For now, I'm going to Europe for a month. Vacations with family. But there's one more topic I want to cover with you before we take a hiatus for a month."

John stretched, a thoughtful expression on his face. "Wow, have fun, Matthew. I've also got a lot to think about in a month."

"You do," Matthew said with a smile. "But it'll all make sense in time. We're just getting started."

As they stepped out of the Gaslamp Museum at the Davis-Horton House, the cool evening air greeted them. The sun had started its descent, casting a warm glow over the historic Victorian architecture. The contrast between the old-world charm of the house and the modern streets of San Diego was striking, but it felt like the perfect backdrop for the conversation they had just wrapped up.

"It's a lot to take in, but it makes sense. I can already see how my perspective on money has been limited. I was just thinking about paychecks and bills, but now…" He trailed off, glancing back at the house. "I see there's so much more."

"That's the point," Matthew nodded. "It's about expanding your view, seeing the bigger picture of what wealth really is and how it's built. You've already taken the first steps."

They paused at the edge of the street, the museum's lanterns flickering to life behind them. A few passersby strolled through the Gaslamp Quarter, enjoying the evening atmosphere. John glanced at his watch and then back at Matthew. "So, we've got one more session before the break?"

"Yep," Matthew confirmed, looking out at the city as if scanning the possibilities ahead. "After that, we'll take a month off, give you time to digest everything. When we pick back up, we'll dive into 'My Hidden Wealth Building Process.' That's where it all comes together."

John smiled. "I'm looking forward to that."

Matthew extended his hand. "You're doing great, John. I'll see you next week."

John took his hand and gave it a firm shake. "Thanks, Matthew. I'll be ready."

With a nod, Matthew turned and walked down the street, disappearing into the flow of the city, leaving John standing there in the fading light, reflecting on how far he had come—and how much further he had to go.

CHAPTER 21

❦

The Winning Attitude

John pulled up to Matthew's home in an affluent neighborhood, where the houses were more like mansions, with sweeping lawns and luxury cars in every driveway. The sheer size of Matthew's home left him speechless. As John stepped out of his car, he took in the grand architecture: clean lines, expansive windows, and a contemporary elegance that blended perfectly with the lavish landscape. The Porsche parked casually in the driveway caught his eye, confirming that Matthew was far beyond comfortable in his financial success.

John approached the front door with excitement and nervousness, not sure what to expect from this last session before their break. The door swung open, and Matthew greeted him with a wide smile.

"Welcome, John," Matthew said, motioning for him to enter. "Come in, make yourself at home."

John stepped inside, his eyes widening at the interior. It was a breathtaking blend of modern luxury and understated style. Large, open spaces, high ceilings, and carefully curated art pieces gave the home a gallery-like feel, while the plush furniture and warm lighting made it feel comfortable, almost intimate. John admired how well everything reflected Matthew's persona—confident, calculated, yet inviting.

Matthew noticed him observing and interrupted his thoughts, "It's a bit much at times, but it serves its purpose." He led John through the spacious hallway to a cozy lounge area with leather sofas and a large marble fireplace. The smell of cedarwood filled the room, and soft jazz played in the background. "Let me fix you a drink," Matthew said as he moved to a sleek bar built into the corner of the room.

John sat down, still processing everything, as Matthew expertly mixed a drink. "I can't believe this is your place," John finally said, shaking his head. "I've never seen anything like it."

Matthew handed him the drink, a subtle smile playing on his lips. "It wasn't always like this, John. I started small, just like everyone else. It's all about making the right moves and staying focused."

They both settled into the lounge, and for a moment, there was a comfortable silence as John took a sip of his drink, savoring the taste. Matthew leaned back and regarded him thoughtfully before breaking the quiet.

"During our sessions," Matthew began, his voice calm and measured, "we've uncovered a lot of the things that hold people back financially. The traps that most fall into, either out of habit or because that's just how they've been taught to live."

John nodded, remembering their previous discussions. "Yeah, like focusing only on income and expenses," he said.

"Exactly," Matthew continued. "I hope you'll use what we've talked about to avoid those traps moving forward. And more than that, I hope you're beginning to see how important it is to be intentional with your money. That's why I suggested you start saving a portion of your monthly income. Even a small amount can make a huge difference in the long run."

Matthew's eyes locked onto John's. "You need capital to make capital. Money doesn't just appear; you have to have some, either yours or borrowed, to get ahead. But more importantly, you have to know how to manage it, and that requires more than just knowledge."

John listened intently, sipping his drink. The atmosphere was warm, but the conversation felt heavier and more serious than usual.

"We always hear that 'knowledge is power,' but that's only half the story," Matthew went on. "There are plenty of financial planners, bankers, and even investors who are just as broke as the average person. They have all the knowledge in the world, but what good is it if they don't know what to do with the money they manage? Financial success isn't just about knowing—it's about acting and acting wisely."

Matthew took a sip from his own glass, pausing for a moment before continuing. "The truth is, money has a way of slipping through the fingers of people who are wasteful or careless. A person's profession or status won't protect them from financial ruin if they have the wrong attitude toward spending."

John shifted in his seat, thinking back to times when he had been guilty of those very habits—spending impulsively and not thinking long-term. "It's hard to break those patterns," he admitted.

"It is," Matthew agreed, "but that's why we're doing this. You need an attitude for success, John. One that not only gets you started but keeps you going, even when it's tough. You have to be relentless if you want to achieve your financial goals. Most people aren't."

Matthew stood and walked toward the large windows overlooking his expansive backyard, where the city lights twinkled in the distance. "You have to become a leader in your own life, not just a follower of what society tells you to do."

John set his glass down, intrigued. "What do you mean?"

Matthew turned back to face him. "Think about it. From the time we're kids, we're shaped by the people around us—our parents, teachers, friends. They mold our beliefs, sometimes for the better, but not always for our individual success. Most of what we learn is designed for the common good, not personal prosperity."

John nodded slowly. "So, we end up following the crowd instead of doing what's best for us."

"Exactly. And that's why most people get stuck in mediocrity. They follow the same script—go to college, get a job, maybe buy a house, and then wonder why they're not financially free." Matthew's voice softened as he sat back down, his gaze steady. "If you want to be exceptional, John, you can't think and act like everyone else. You need to believe in your unique abilities and follow your own path, even if it means stepping away from what's 'normal.'"

John sipped the drink Matthew had made for him—a simple but potent cocktail. His hands wrapped around the glass, trying to process everything he was hearing. Matthew's home was not just a display of wealth; it was the result of discipline, focus, and the kind of hard-earned success Matthew was now laying out for him.

"Your thinking, mannerisms, and work ethic must be exceptionally higher than the average person's," Matthew said, his voice calm but firm. "This is because your purpose demands it. You're willing to do whatever it takes to succeed, right?"

John nodded. He had always considered himself hardworking, but Matthew was pushing him beyond what he thought he was capable of.

"When you decide to lead your life," Matthew continued, leaning forward slightly, "people will test your courage. Even the ones closest to you—your family, your friends—will challenge your resolve. And when they do, your belief and self-confidence must be strong enough to withstand their criticisms."

John shifted in his seat, thinking of all the people who had doubted his choices in the past. Could he really stand firm in the face of that pressure?

Matthew seemed to sense his unease. "You've got to stand tall because you're a leader, John. Leaders aren't born; they're made. You have everything it takes to become one. All that's required is a simple decision that says, 'I'm gonna do this,' and then you apply the actions to make it happen."

He let the words hang in the air for a moment before adding, "If you need training, get it. If you need to relocate, move. And if you need money, find a way to get it—legally."

John smiled at that, appreciating the emphasis. Matthew wasn't one to suggest shortcuts or dishonesty. Everything he had achieved was through discipline, and that same integrity was expected from him.

"Look," Matthew said, "if you're having difficulty finding money to save, there are things you can start doing today. Cut back on dining out—people don't realize how much they blow on restaurants. And as for groceries, focus on eating healthier. Fruits and vegetables are cheaper than meat and keep you alive longer." He chuckled, breaking the tension in the room.

John nodded, feeling a sense of relief. This wasn't just about making huge leaps overnight. It was about practical, steady steps.

"Buy a reliable car, not an expensive one. Brew your coffee at home instead of buying it on the way to work. These are small habits, but they add up."

Matthew's tone shifted, becoming more serious again. "The heart of the matter is this, John: you have to get rid of personal and cultural habits that hold you back. There's nothing wrong with enjoying life, but catering to every whim keeps people in debt. I've seen it too many times—people buying things just because they're on sale or getting sucked into holiday shopping sprees. It's all unnecessary."

John stared at the liquid in his glass, feeling the truth of Matthew's words. He could already see areas in his own life where he could make changes.

Matthew continued, "Most leaders I know have worked and sacrificed to become who they are. You've seen it with your own eyes. Nature has a way of rewarding those who are truly committed. And you, John, will be blessed for your courage and your hard work if you accept these challenges."

Matthew paused, letting the quiet return for a moment as they both gazed out the window. The sun had begun to set, turning a soft glow of pink over the skyline. John took it in, imagining the future Matthew was describing—a future where he was no longer bogged down by financial stress, where he could make the kinds of decisions that led to real success.

"Don't let circumstances or negative emotions get in your way," Matthew said, his voice steady but commanding. "It's easy to look at your current situation—whether it's your finances, your living conditions, your education—and think that's all there is. But leaders, John, they don't have time for that kind of thinking."

"What kind of emotions do you mean?" John asked, leaning in slightly. He knew he wasn't immune to those kinds of traps.

Matthew smiled, a knowing look in his eyes. "Self-pity, for one. You know, when things don't go your way, it's easy to feel sorry for yourself. But leaders don't wallow in disappointment. They accept it and move on."

John felt a knot tighten in his stomach. He'd been guilty of that—dwelling on setbacks instead of pushing forward.

"Then there's procrastination," Matthew said, his tone sharpening. "It'll harm anyone if they let it. You've got to get things done, John. Also, no excuses. And speaking of excuses, those are just defense mechanisms people use to cover their own fears. Don't make them. Just make progress."

John felt a surge of motivation rise in him. Matthew's words were cutting through all the noise in his head, the doubts and excuses that had held him back.

"Complaining? That's another trap. Leaders don't waste time complaining. Life is full of ups and downs, but you can't focus on the negatives."

The room seemed to fade away as John absorbed the final piece of advice. Matthew had laid out a path—not just to financial success but to a life of leadership and purpose. It was clear, now more than ever, that this wasn't just about making money. It was about becoming the kind of man who could shape his life as he saw fit.

Matthew leaned in, "Stay focused," he said, locking eyes with John. "The world is filled with pessimists— people who expect the worst and will try to convince you that your path is too risky, too uncertain. They'll make you second-guess yourself, but leaders don't have the luxury of entertaining those doubts."

John nodded, though his brow furrowed. He was thinking of all the times friends or even family members had dismissed his ideas, urging him to play it safe. He could see their faces now, and Matthew seemed to notice the conflict in his expression.

"Look," Matthew continued, softening his tone, "you can't waste time worrying about what might go wrong. A leader's job is to keep moving forward, even when the odds are against him. Even when things seem hopeless.

You have a mission, John, and you have to stay focused on that—no matter what."

"How do you do that?" John asked, a bit of uncertainty creeping into his voice. "How do you stay focused when the world is telling you you're wrong?"

Matthew smiled knowingly as if he'd heard this question a hundred times before. "Sometimes, staying focused means cutting out the clutter—the noise, the distractions, even some people. It's about simplifying your life so you can put all your energy into what really matters. I'll tell you something I've learned over the years: people will always have opinions. But their opinions are none of your business."

John smirked. "Easier said than done."

"True," Matthew said, "but that's where discipline comes in. And here are a few tips to help you maintain that focus: First, believe in your ability. You're capable of so much more than you think. You just need to tap into that inner strength. Push yourself beyond your comfort zone because that's where real growth happens."

"Second," Matthew's voice grew more intense, "you need to take risks. Without risk, there is no reward. The most successful people I know didn't get there by playing it safe. They sacrificed, took risks, and made it happen."

John looked thoughtful, recalling times he had hesitated to take a leap, fearing the consequences. He nodded slowly.

"Next," Matthew continued, "you must cultivate good friendships. Avoid the energy suckers—you know who I mean. The ones who complain, who lack ambition, and who always have something negative to say. Instead, surround yourself with people who inspire and challenge you to be better. People who push you to your highest potential."

John glanced down, thinking of some of the people in his life who always seemed to drain him, even though he loved them. He made a mental note to reassess those relationships.

"And this one is key," Matthew added, raising a finger for emphasis. "You have to trust in God. No matter how strong you are, there's a limit to what you can do on your own. There's a force greater than all of us—God Almighty. Trust him, and he will guide you through every challenge."

John's lips pressed together as he processed this. He wasn't deeply religious, but he understood the value of faith—especially in uncertain times.

"Another important aspect," Matthew went on, "is admitting your weaknesses. Don't be afraid to tell your partner, your kids, or even your closest friends when you're struggling. That vulnerability isn't a weakness— it's a strength. It builds character, fosters trust, and ultimately makes you a better leader."

"I'm not sure I'm ready for that," John confessed. "I've always felt like I had to keep it together."

"You don't have to be perfect," Matthew assured him. "In fact, admitting that you're not perfect is what will make you stronger. And finally, act now. There's no time like the present. Every second you wait is another opportunity lost. As Churchill once said, 'I like things to happen, and if they don't happen, I like to make them happen.' The world doesn't wait for us, John. You have to make your move."

John exhaled, feeling the weight of Matthew's words. "It sounds like a complete mindset shift."

"It is," Matthew replied. 'Changing your thinking isn't easy, but it's necessary. Culture has trained us to live a certain way, to think small, to be satisfied with less. But you have to undo all of that. You have to see past your circumstances and start thinking about what's possible."

There was a brief pause before Matthew leaned forward, his voice low but powerful. "You must also refuse to accept the financial limitations imposed on you by society."

John's brow raised. "What do you mean?"

"In the previous sessions," Matthew explained, "we talked about how your career can dictate your financial reality. A young man with no degree working in a warehouse—he's stuck in a system that undervalues him. He may make $10 to $17 an hour, and for the moment, that might be fine. But here's the thing: there's no reason for him to stay there forever."

John nodded. "Yeah, but not everyone has the opportunity to just break out of that."

"True," Matthew agreed. "But that's where the difference in mindset comes in. You don't resign yourself to a limited outcome. You start thinking bigger. Maybe you hold onto that job for now, but in your free time, you look for ways to increase your value—whether through education, experience, or something else."

"And if education isn't an option?" John pressed.

Matthew chuckled softly. "Then you start thinking outside the box. Don't get me wrong, education is great, but it's not the only way to increase your worth. Some people think it is too small and focused on hourly wages. But why limit yourself to $20 or $30 an hour? Why not $100 or even $300 an hour?"

John's eyes widened. "That seems... far-fetched."

"Only if you believe it is," Matthew countered. "That's the problem. The difference between someone who makes $15 an hour and someone who makes $150 an hour is often just in the way they think. People who think big open doors that others can't even see. If you believe you're worth more, you'll find a way to make it happen. But if you limit yourself, if you accept that $35 an hour is your ceiling, then that's exactly where you'll stay. The mind is a powerful thing, John. Start thinking bigger, and the rest will follow."

The room grew quiet as John pondered the possibilities, the gears in his mind turning. Finally, he looked at Matthew and said, "I guess it's time to start thinking big."

Matthew looked at John and opened his mouth to emphasize the importance of his next words. "Also, Stay on course, John. It's easy to get excited about something new—full of energy and motivation surging through your veins—and then, a day or two later, that passion fades. It's human nature. We've all seen it. Think of people at rallies, for example. They leave those events charged up, ready to change the world, but within days, that fire dims. They lose momentum, and before they know it, they're back where they started, waiting for another rally to reignite the flame."

John nodded, reflecting on moments in his own life where initial excitement had fizzled out. He could see the truth in Matthew's words.

Matthew continued, "Losing excitement while pursuing a goal is natural. What separates success from failure is what you do when that passion fades. You have to keep going, even when things seem to be falling apart. You might face delays, family issues, even health problems—maybe something more severe like death. Nothing in life is guaranteed. That's why you have to anticipate the roadblocks and keep moving forward, no matter what."

John looked down, running his hand over the worn armrest of the chair. "It's tough though, isn't it? Sometimes, you don't even see those obstacles coming."

"It is tough," Matthew agreed, his voice firm but encouraging. "But that's why you have to stay focused, stay on course. Life is like flying an airplane—you're constantly adjusting the course because turbulence or wind will push you off track. The pilot doesn't panic when the plane veers slightly. He just corrects it. Same with your financial journey. Point A to point B—no straight lines, but as long as you keep your eye on the destination, you'll get there."

John looked up, absorbing the analogy. "So, what do you do when it gets hard? When you're just not feeling it?"

Matthew smiled, leaning back in his chair. "You keep going anyway. You find inspiration wherever you can. Surround yourself with things that remind you of why you started this journey in the first place. And think BIG, John. Imagine your success in exaggerated terms. Envision what your life will look like when you reach your goals. Scientists say the mind can't tell the difference between real and imagined, so let your mind work for you. Picture that life vividly."

John chuckled, shaking his head. "Exaggerate, huh?"

"Yes, exaggerate," Matthew replied, his smile widening. "And once you've reached your goal, don't let anyone pull you away from your vision. You'll find people trying to push you in a thousand different directions. But this wealth-building journey you're on—it's your project. Own it, drive it, and make sure it benefits you and your family."

The room seemed to hum with energy as Matthew finished. He paused, allowing his words to sink in, then extended his hand to John. "Until we meet again, I wish you Godspeed and great success."

John grasped Matthew's hand firmly, feeling the weight of the journey ahead but also the strength of the resolve he had built over these sessions.

***

As John left their wealth-building session, he couldn't help but feel a growing sense of clarity. Each time he met with Matthew, it was like another layer of fog lifted, revealing a clearer path toward the American Dream he'd always envisioned. But it wasn't just about business or making deals—it was about understanding the mechanics behind wealth itself. John had been learning that even those with meager incomes could get ahead. They didn't need to start with much, just the right knowledge and mindset.

And there was something else Matthew had teased during their conversation—a secret strategy. John felt a surge of excitement at the thought of it. Matthew called it the "Wealth Builder System." He had promised that this system was the key, the hidden strategy that could propel anyone to financial success, regardless of where they started.

John felt anticipation building within him. What was this secret? What was this hidden knowledge that Matthew kept just out of reach? He couldn't wait to find out.

But for now, he had enough. Enough to start. Enough to begin making changes in his life, to begin the process of financial freedom.

As he drove away from Matthew's home, John felt more than just hopeful—he felt empowered, ready to take control of his financial future.

About the Author

❦

Tom Graneau, a certified financial educator, licensed life insurance agent, family counselor, and ordained minister explores the intersection of faith, finances, and family dynamics for personal growth and spiritual vibrancy. His books entertain, educate, and inspire, offering practical insights into financial strategies, spiritual vision, and perception. Whether seeking financial wisdom, spiritual guidance, or helpful life advice, Tom Graneau' s work is valuable on your journey toward personal success and spiritual fulfillment.

www.ingramcontent.com/pod-product-compliance
Lightning Source LLC
Chambersburg PA
CBHW071542210326
41597CB00019B/3088